New Rules of
Sociological Method

New Rules of Sociological Method

A Positive Critique of
Interpretative Sociologies

Anthony Giddens

Second Edition

Stanford University Press
Stanford, California
1993

Stanford University Press
Stanford, California
© 1993 Anthony Giddens
First published by Hutchinson, 1976.
Second, revised edition first published 1993
    by Polity Press in association with Blackwell Publishers.
First published in the U.S.A. by
    Stanford University Press, 1993
Printed in Great Britain
Cloth ISBN 0-8047-2225-0
Paper ISBN 0-8047-2226-9
LC 93-83809
This book is printed on acid-free paper.

Contents

Preface

This study is only intended as one part of a more embracing project. While it can of course be read as a self-contained work, it touches upon various issues that are not dealt with in a detailed way, but which are vital to my project as a whole. This latter involves three overlapping concerns. One is to develop a critical approach to the development of nineteenth-century social theory, and its subsequent incorporation as the institutionalized and professionalized 'disciplines' of 'sociology', 'anthropology' and 'political science' in the course of the twentieth century. Another is to trace out some of the main themes in nineteenth-century social thought which became built into theories of the formation of the advanced societies and subject these to critique. The third is to elaborate upon, and similarly to begin a reconstruction of, problems raised by the – always troubling – character of the social sciences as concerned with, as a 'subject-matter', what those 'sciences' themselves presuppose: human social activity and intersubjectivity. This book is proposed as a contribution to the last of these three. But any such discussion bursts the bounds of this sort of conceptual container, and has immediate implications for work in the other areas. As a single project, they are tied together as an endeavour to construct a critical analysis of the legacy of the social theory of the nineteenth and early twentieth centuries for the contemporary period.

This book is about 'method' in the sense in which social philosophers characteristically employ the term – the sense in which Durkheim used it in his *Rules of Sociological Method*. That is to say, it is not a guide to 'how to do practical research', and does not offer any specific research proposals. It is primarily an exercise in clarification of logical issues. I have subtitled the study a 'positive critique' of 'interpretative sociologies'. Anyone who reads on will see that this does not mean 'positivistic'. I use it only to mean 'sympathetic' or 'constructive': the sense that predates Comte's translation of the term into a definite philosophy of social and natural science. 'Interpretative sociologies' is something of a misnomer for the schools of thought that appear in the first chapter, since some of the authors whose work is discussed there are anxious to separate what they have to say from 'sociology'. I use the term only because there is no other readily available one, to group together a series of writings that have certain shared concerns with 'meaningful action'.

The themes of this study are that social theory must incorporate a treatment of action as rationalized conduct ordered reflexively by human agents, and must grasp the significance of language as the practical medium whereby this is made possible. The implications of these notions are profound, and the book is confined to tracing through only some of them. Anyone who recognizes that self-reflection, as mediated linguistically, is integral to the characterization of human social conduct must acknowledge that such holds also for his or her own activities as a social 'analyst', 'researcher', etc. I think it correct to say, moreover, that theories produced in the social sciences are not just 'meaning frames' in their own right, but also constitute moral interventions in the social life whose conditions of existence they seek to clarify.

Introduction to the Second Edition

Quite a number of years have passed since this book first saw the light of day, but I hope it has not lost its relevance to current problems of social theory. In *New Rules* I deal with a number of forms of interpretative sociology, as well as with certain more central sociological traditions. When I wrote it, I regarded the book – and continue to do so today – as a 'dialogic critique' of the forms of social and philosophical thought which it addresses. That is, it is a critical engagement with ideas that I see as of essential importance, but which for one reason or another were not adequately developed in the perspectives from which they originally sprang. Some have seen such a strategy as a misplaced eclecticism, but I consider such dialogic critique as the very life-blood of fruitful conceptual development in social theory.

New Rules of Sociological Method dovetails with other 'positive critiques' which I sought to provide in elaborating the basic tenets of structuration theory. In complementary writings that I undertook at about the same period, I addressed approaches to social analysis either left aside, or treated only in a marginal way, in *New Rules*. Such approaches included naturalistic sociology – a term which I now think of as preferable to the more diffuse and ambiguous label, 'positivism' – functionalism, structuralism and 'post-structuralism'. *The Constitution of Society* (1984) established a more comprehensive framework for the notion of structuration than was available in *New Rules*, but did not supplant it.[1] *New Rules* makes an independent statement about questions of agency, structure and social transformation; its distinctive concentration is upon the nature of 'action' and the implications of an analysis of action for the logic of social science.

The debates have moved on over the period since *New Rules* was originally published, but in revising the text I have found little of substance that I think it necessary to abandon or reformulate. The work of Talcott Parsons still has its adherents and, as filtered through the writings of Niklas Luhmann and others, remains influential; but it no longer has the central position it once held. Phenomenological notions are not as widely drawn upon now as they were at the time, while post-structuralism, in its different guises, has increased its importance and has become allied to conceptions of post-modernism. I do not feel, however, that these changes make any substantial difference to the standpoint I developed in this study, which retains its validity.

New Rules has attracted its own share of critiques, some positive and others more destructive in impetus. I have responded to such criticism in a variety of places and shall not cover the same ground again here. Let me concentrate upon two issues only: whether or not the idea of the 'duality of structure', vital to structuration theory, merges levels of social life that should be kept apart; and whether the distinction between the 'single hermeneutic' of natural science and the 'double hermeneutic' of the social sciences should be sustained. The literature subsequent to the publication of *New Rules* contains many discussions of these problems. For purposes of simplicity, I shall focus upon those offered by Nicos Mouzelis in respect of the first question, and Hans Harbers and Gerard de Vries in respect of the second.[2]

Many critics have accepted the objections I made against the concept of structure as ordinarily used in sociology. Seen as 'fixed' and, in Durkheimian fashion, as 'external' to social actors, it appears as a constraint upon action, rather than also as enabling. It is to grasp this double character that I introduced the notion of the duality of structure. What are some of the objections that might be levelled against it? They include the following.

1   It may be true that actors routinely draw upon rules and
    resources, and thereby reproduce them, in the course of their
    day-to-day activities. Surely, however, such an orientation
    to rules and resources is not the only, or even the predomin-
    ant, one they have? For, as Mouzelis puts it, 'Actors often
    distance themselves from rules and resources, in order to
    question them, or in order to build theories about them, or –
    even more importantly – in order to devise strategies for
    either their maintenance or their transformation.'[3]

2   Hence it follows that the idea of the duality of structure
    cannot properly account for the constitution or reproduction
    of social systems. Rules and resources are reproduced not
    only in the context of their practical use, but also where
    actors 'distance' themselves from them in order to treat them
    in a strategic way. When such a circumstance applies, the
    concept of the duality of structure is quite inappropriate.
    Instead, perhaps, we should speak of a *dualism*, because the
    individual, the 'subject', confronts rules and resources as
    'objects' in the social environment.

3   These comments bear directly upon distinctions between
    micro- and macro-analysis in the social sciences. Although
    not discussed directly in *New Rules*, the micro/macro dif-
    ferentiation, as ordinarily understood, is something which I
    place in question. However, if we try to do without it, the
    critic asserts, the result is an illegitimate reductionism. Social
    systems have many structural properties which cannot be
    understood in terms of the actions of situated individuals.
    Micro- and macro-analysis are not mutually exclusive; each
    in fact requires the other, but they have to be kept apart.

4   The idea of the duality of structure cannot cope with action
    oriented to large- rather than small-scale contexts. For
    instance, it may work well when one considers an everyday
    conversation between two people in the street, but does not
    fit a situation where, say, a group of heads of state meet to
    take decisions affecting millions. The former situation, it
    might be said , is inconsequential in its implications for larger
    social orders, while the latter affects such orders in a direct
    and comprehensive way. In structuration theory there is an
    'identification' of agency with 'micro-subjects which, by the

routine use of rules and resources, contribute to the reproduction of the institutional order. Macro action is neglected –
both the type of action that results from the incumbency of
authority positions . . . as well as that which results from the
variable ability of individual subjects to group together in
order to defend, maintain, or transform rules and resources.'[4]

5 The Durkheimian notions of externality and constraint need
to be sustained, albeit perhaps not in the form in which
Durkheim himself expressed them. There are degrees or
levels involved; what is external and constraining for one
individual may be much less so for another. This point connects with the previous ones, for it means recognizing that
social life is hierarchical – rather than speaking of 'the individual' confronting 'society', we should acknowledge a multi-
plicity of levels of social organization, with varying degrees of
disjunction between them.

In responding to such observations, let me first of all expand
upon why I developed the concept of duality of structure. I did
so in order to contest two main types of dualism. One is that
found among pre-existing theoretical perspectives. Interpretative
sociologies, such as those discussed in *New Rules*, as I have put
it elsewhere, are 'strong on action, but weak on structure'. They
see human beings as purposive agents, who are aware of themselves as such and have reasons for what they do; but they
have little means of coping with issues which quite rightly bulk
large in functionalist and structural approaches – problems
of constraint, power and large-scale social organization. This
second group of approaches, on the other hand, while 'strong on
structure', has been 'weak on action'. Agents are treated as if
they were inert and inept – the playthings of forces larger than
themselves.

In breaking away from such a dualism of theoretical perspectives, the analysis developed in *New Rules* also rejects the
dualism of 'the individual' and 'society'. Neither forms a proper
starting-point for theoretical reflection; instead the focus is upon
reproduced practices. It is important, however, to be clear about
what discarding the dualism of 'the individual'/'society' means.
It emphatically does not mean denying that there are social

systems and forms of collectivity which have their own distinct structural properties. Nor does it imply that those properties are somehow 'contained' in the actions of each situated individual. To challenge the dualism of the individual and society is to insist that each should be *deconstructed.*

Since 'the individual' has corporeal existence, the concept might seem unproblematic. Yet an individual is not a body and even the notion of the body, in relation to the acting self, turns out to be complex. To speak of an individual is to speak not just of a 'subject', but also of an agent; the idea of action (as Talcott Parsons always stressed) is thus inevitably a central one. Moreover – and this is crucial – action is not simply a quality of the individual but is, equally, the stuff of social organization or collective life as well. Most sociologists, including even many working within frameworks of interpretative sociology, have failed to recognize that social theory, no matter how 'macro' its concerns, demands a sophisticated understanding of agency and the agent just as much as it does an account of the complexities of society. It is precisely such an understanding that *New Rules* seeks to develop.

The concept of the duality of structure is bound up with the logic of social analysis; it does not, in and of itself, offer any generalizations about the conditions of social reproduction/ transformation. This point is fundamental, because otherwise a structurationist view would indeed be open to the charge of reductionism. To say that the production and reproduction of social life are one and the same thing takes *no* position at all about the conditions of stability or change in concrete conditions of social activity. Rather, it is to say that neither on the level of logic, nor in our practical day-to-day lives, can we step outside the flow of action, whether such action contributes to the most rigid of social institutions or to the most radical forms of social change.

These things having been said, I can comment upon points 1–5 in sequence. Point 1 both misunderstands the notion of duality of structure and presumes too primitive a concept of reflexivity. All actors are social theorists, and must be so to be social agents at all. The conventions which are drawn upon in the organization of social life are never 'blind habits'. One of the distinctive contributions of phenomenology, and particularly of ethno-methodology, has been to show that (1) the conduct of social life continually involves 'theorizing' and (2) even the most enduring of habits, or the most unshakeable of social norms, involves continual and detailed reflexive attention. Routinization is of elemental importance in social life; but all routines, all the time, are contingent and potentially fragile accomplishments.

Individuals in all forms of society 'distance themselves' from rules and resources, approach them strategically and so forth. In some respects, for reasons just noted, this is the condition of even the most regularized modes of social reproduction. No matter how traditional a context of action, for example, tradition is chronically interpreted, reinterpreted, generalized about, as the very means whereby it is 'done'. Of course, all moments of reflexive attention themselves draw upon, and reconstitute, rules and resources; to repeat, there can be no stepping outside of the flow of action.

The sort of 'distancing' Mouzelis has in mind, however, is particularly evident in social circumstances where the hold of tradition has become attenuated. A useful distinction can be drawn here between reflexivity, as a quality of human action as a whole, and *institutional reflexivity*, as an historical phenomenon. Institutional reflexivity refers to the institutionalization of an investigative and calculative attitude towards generalized conditions of system reproduction; it both stimulates and reflects a decline in traditional ways of doing things. It is also associated with the generation of power (understood as transformative capacity). The expansion of institutional reflexivity stands behind the proliferation of organizations in circumstances of modernity, including organizations of global scope.[5]

So far as point 2 goes, I should reaffirm that the duality of structure 'accounts for' nothing. It has explanatory value only when we consider real historical situations of some sort. The 'duality' of the duality of structure concerns the dependence of action and structure, taken as a logical assertion, but it certainly does not involve a merging of the situated actor with the collectivity. Much better here, indeed, to speak of a hierarchy rather than the sustaining of a dualism: there are many modes of interconnection between individuals and collectivities. It is perfectly obvious that every situated actor faces an environment of action which has an 'objectivity' for him or her in a quasi-Durkheimian sense.

As for points 3 and 4, the distinction between micro- and macro-analysis is not a very useful one in social science, at least in some of the ways in which it is ordinarily understood. It is especially misleading if seen itself as a dualism – where 'micro-situations' are those to which a notion of agency is appropriate, whereas 'macro-situations' are those over which individuals have no control.[6] What is important is to consider the ties, as well as the disjunctions, between situations of co-presence and 'mediated connections' between individuals and collectivities of various types. It is just not the case that what Mouzelis calls 'macro action' is left aside in structuration theory. 'Macro action', however, for the reasons he gives, is not the same as lack of co-presence: here the phenomenon of differential power is usually central. A small number of individuals meeting together may enact policies that have very extensive consequences. Macro-action of this sort is even more pervasive than Mouzelis implies, because it is by no means limited to conscious processes of decision-making; large-scale systems of power are reproduced just as strongly in more routinized circumstances of co-present interaction.

As for point 5, social life, particularly in conditions of modernity, does involve multiple levels of collective activity. Far from being inconsistent with the views set out in *New Rules*, such an observation is entirely in line with them. 'Externality' and 'constraint' cannot be seen, as Durkheim thought, as general characteristics of 'social facts'. 'Constraint' takes several forms, some of which again concern the phenomenon of differential power. The 'externality' of social facts does not define them *as* social facts, but instead directs attention to various different properties/contexts/levels of the environments of action of situated individuals.

In structuration theory, the concept of 'structure' presumes that of 'system': it is only social systems or collectivities which have structural properties. Structure derives above all from regularized practices and is hence closely tied to institutionalization; structure gives *form* to totalizing influences in social life.

Is it then in the end misleading to try to illuminate the conception of the duality of structure by reference to language use? It is misleading, I think, if we see language as a closed and homogeneous entity. Rather, we should conceive of language as a fragmented and diverse array of practices, contexts and modes of collective organization. As I stress in the text, the idea of Lévi-Strauss, that 'society is like a language', should be resisted strongly; but the study of language certainly helps cast light upon some basic characteristics of social activity as a whole.

All this having been said, the critic may still feel worried or dissatisfied. For is there not a long distance between 'everyday practices', the situated interaction of individuals, and the properties of the large-scale, even global, social systems that influence so much of modern social life? How could the former in any way be the medium of the reproduction of the structural properties of the latter? One response to this question would be to say that, as a result of current globalizing trends, there actually *are* very important respects in which everyday activities connect to global outcomes and vice versa. In the global economy, for example, local purchasing decisions affect, and serve to constitute, economic orders which in turn act back upon subsequent decisions. The type of food a person eats is globally consequential in respect of global ecology. On a somewhat less encompassing level, the way in which a man looks at a woman may be a constituting element of deeply engrained structures of gender power. The reproduction/transformation of globalizing systems is implicated in a whole variety of day-to-day decisions and acts.

Deconstructing 'society', however, means recognizing the basic significance of diversity, context and history. Processes of empirical social reproduction intersect with one another in many different ways in relation to their time–space 'stretch', to the generation and distribution of power, and to institutional reflexivity. The proper locus for the study of social reproduction is in the immediate process of the constituting of interaction, for all social life is an active accomplishment; and every moment of social life bears the imprint of the totality. 'The totality', however, is not an inclusive, bounded 'society', but a composite of diverse totalizing orders and impulsions.

Institutional reflexivity – this notion connects the analysis of

modernity with the more generalized idea of the double hermeneutic. The 'double' of the 'double hermeneutic' again implies a duality: the 'findings' of social science do not remain
insulated from the 'subject-matter' to which they refer, but
consistently re-enter and reshape it. It is of the first importance
to emphasize that what is at issue here is not the existence of
feed-back mechanisms. On the contrary, the intrusion of concepts and knowledge-claims back into the universe of events
they were coined to describe produces an essential erraticism.
The double hermeneutic is thus intrinsically involved in the
dislocated, fragmenting nature of modernity as such, particularly
in the phase of 'high modernity'.[7]

Many implications flow from this observation, but I shall consider the thesis of the double hermeneutic here only from the
point of view of recent debates in the philosophy and sociology
of science. Such debates have their origins in the by-now
accepted observation that natural science has hermeneutic traits.
As discussed in *New Rules*, the old differentiation between
Verstehen and *Erklären* has become problematic; the idea that
natural science deals only, or even primarily, in law-like
generalization belongs to a view of scientific activity which has
now largely become abandoned. As Karen Knorr-Cetina puts it,
'Natural science investigation is grounded in the same kind of
situational logic and marked by the same kind of indexical
reasoning which we used to associate with the symbolic and
interactional character of the social world.'[8]

Such conclusions have been reached as a result of sociological
studies of science rather than philosophical interpretation. Thus
experimentation, long considered the bedrock of scientific knowledge, has been studied as a process of the translation and
construction of contextual information. But is this a 'single
hermeneutic' which can be differentiated from the double
hermeneutic of natural science? Some, including Knorr-Cetina,
claim not. This distinction, she says, depends upon two assumptions: that human beings possess 'causal agency' not found in
nature; and that, in the social world, there is a distinctive means,
conscious appropriation, whereby causal agency is triggered.
Neither is justified. The first rests upon too unsophisticated a
notion of natural causality, for objects in the natural world may

also be said to possess causal powers. The second ignores the fact that there are equivalent, if not directly parallel, triggering mechanisms for the reception of information in the world of nature.

Harbers and de Vries suggest that these conflicting views of the double hermeneutic can be looked at in the light of empirical evidence. Knorr-Cetina bases her thesis upon historical and so-ciological studies of natural science. Why not consider in a direct way the influence of social science within broader frameworks of knowledge and action? According to them, the thesis of the double hermeneutic presumes two hypotheses: that where the common-sense interpretations constituting social phenomena become the subject of historical change, interpretations offered within the social sciences will change correspondingly; and that novel concepts or findings developed within social science will have to be defended not only within the sociological community but in relation to a 'common-sense forum of lay individuals'. The notion of the double hermeneutic implies that, in contrast to the situation in natural science, sociologists have a 'scientific', rather than only civic, obligation to present their ideas to a lay audi-ence.[9] Harbers and de Vries examine these hypotheses by look-ing at developments in education in The Netherlands.

Sociologists have long been involved in documenting unequal educational opportunities. Many projects were established in different countries from the 1950s onwards in order to uncover the factors influencing such inequalities. The Dutch Project on Talents was one of these, the work of a group of eleven social investigators. The idea of the research was to study the large reserve of 'unused talents' believed to exist. In other words, it was thought that many children from poorer backgrounds were qualified for advanced levels of secondary education, but were not to be found in the appropriate schools. The results did not conform to this expectation. Children attended schools which matched their abilities; the relative under-representation of children from underprivileged backgrounds was not because of misdirected decisions about type of school after primary education. The children had already lagged behind in primary school.

These conclusions were at first accepted by most educational authorities and government policy became based on them. Subsequently, however, another researcher published a book using new calculations derived from the same data. Using a different concept of 'talent', he concluded that a reserve of unusual talents did indeed exist. The original Project on Talents had been carried out within a definite framework of assumptions corresponding to a popular view of what a 'meritocracy' is. The second researcher attacked those assumptions, and proposed not only a different view of educational equality but a different practical orientation to reducing it. His concepts and findings contributed to a dissolution of the 'meritocratic consensus' that previously existed. In turn, the sociology of education produced new definitions of research problems and became divided into a number of opposing perspectives. These then in their turn were filtered back into public debates on educational policy issues.

Harbers and de Vries suggest that their study provides a concrete example of the double hermeneutic: public attitudes on education were altered by, and helped alter, processes of social research. Where the 'theoretical style' of research work is consonant with widely held lay assumptions, they say, common-sense assumptions remain unnoticed by all parties. In such a situation, the sociological investigator can appear as an 'autonomous scientist', much like the natural scientist. Where a variety of dissident opinions exists among the lay public, however, claims about analyses of social phenomena have to be put forward and defended simultaneously in different forums. They conclude:

> social scientists are dependent upon common sense thinking in a way which is strikingly different from the relation between common sense and scientific knowledge in the natural sciences. Whereas, of course, in the latter ideas, concepts, metaphors, etcetera may be adopted from non-scientific traditions and, hence, common sense thinking may serve as a resource, common sense interpretations set limits to the social sciences and constrain their cognitive development along the lines set out in the hypotheses we have formulated.[10]

The view of Harbers and de Vries has been criticized by William Lynch, who defends a view close to that of Knorr-Cetina.[11] The social and natural sciences are after all not so different; but to see this we must concentrate more upon natural than social science. Thus an interaction between accounts of a subject-matter and 'responses' from that subject-matter occurs in the natural as well as the social world. In social life, actors' accounts are often, even normally, 'represented' – some people, who remain silent, are spoken for by others. The same happens in natural science where scientists or lay actors 'speak for' the natural world. Similarly, the causal order of natural reality is altered by accounts imposed on it. For the natural world is not an inert, pre-given object, but is itself 'constituted' by the accounts scientists and lay agents provide.

Consider the phenomenon of deductive-nomological laws in the natural sciences. Such laws, Lynch says, 'do not hold in the real world'. Rather, they depend upon elaborate interventions which scientists make into the natural order to establish the conditions under which such laws can be 'seen to hold'. To 'extend' such laws outside the laboratory usually implies constructing conditions in which law-like behaviour can be 'appropriately manifested'. Such laws 'depend for their applicability on closed conditions that never fully obtain and require intervention and manipulation for their demonstration'.[12]

If natural scientists are able to claim greater autonomy than their counterparts in the social sciences, this is largely because of the degree to which a culture favourable to scientific claims has developed in modern societies. A great deal of work has gone into ensuring that natural scientists are less accountable than their social-scientific colleagues for their epistemic choices. Focusing on a double hermeneutic only in social science, therefore, reinforces a well-established tendency to obscure the cognitive and practical impact which natural science has upon the lives of lay individuals. The double hermeneutic, as applied specifically to social science, proscribes 'empirical examination of past lay constraints on natural scientific development and, potentially, further interventions in issues for which the public might claim to have a stake'.[13]

To assess the validity of these ideas it is necessary to go over some of the ground covered in *New Rules* about the concept of the double hermeneutic – in respect not just of the meaning of 'double' but also of that of 'hermeneutic'. The idea of the double hermeneutic is partly a logical and partly an empirical one. All social science is irretrievably hermeneutic in the sense that to be able to describe 'what someone is doing' in any given context means knowing what the agent or agents themselves know, and apply, in the constitution of their activities. It is being able (in principle) to 'go on' – mutual knowledge shared by participants and social-scientific observers. The hermeneutic element involved here does not have a parallel in natural science, which does not deal with knowledgeable agents in such a way – even in the case of most animal behaviour.

This is the logical side of the double hermeneutic. Lay actors are concept-bearing beings, whose concepts enter constitutively into what they do; the concepts of social science cannot be kept insulated from their potential appropriation and incorporation within everyday action. The empirical side concerns institutional reflexivity, a phenomenon which, as noted previously, becomes particularly pervasive with the maturation of the modern social order. The social sciences are deeply involved in the institutional reflexivity of modernity, although they far from exhaust it. As an empirical phenomenon, institutional reflexivity lends itself to research study, although in this regard certain provisos must be made. There is no way of standing wholly apart from reflexivity, since the social-scientific observer, by making her or his results public, relinquishes control over them. The ambition of blunting institutional reflexivity by means of preventing the self-fulfilling or self-negating prophecy, as *New Rules* makes clear, is a futile one; not because research cannot sometimes take account of them, but because they are seen as contaminations of the research process, rather than as intrinsic to the relation between social science and its 'subject-matter'.

Is there any virtue in the sort of study carried out by Harbers and de Vries? There is, I think, as a case-study of certain processes of institutional reflexivity; but fresh empirical research is not needed, in my view, to document that the double hermeneutic actually exists. Institutional reflexivity is so central to modernity that a myriad of examples of it could be offered. The double hermeneutic is much more complex, and less narrowly bounded, than Harbers and de Vries assume in their formulation. There is no necessary match between changing common-sense interpretations of social phenomena and the ideas and theories of social science. Many different connections and oppositions between these are possible. The findings of social science do, in my view, have to be defended *vis-à-vis* those whose activities they cover, and others also; but this is primarily an ethical/political issue, because of the claim to 'know better' than lay agents themselves why things happen as they do.

These considerations do not resolve the question of whether there is a double hermeneutic in natural science. If such were the case, we should have a new version of the 'unity of the sciences', albeit one which differs greatly from the old naturalistic view. Since *New Rules* was written, constructivist and ethnomethodological accounts of natural science have developed apace and, apart perhaps from their more eccentric fringes, have contributed much to the emergence of a sophisticated sociological understanding of science. I do not believe, however, that they compromise the views set out here. The 'single hermeneutic' of science should not be equated with its autonomy in respect of lay beliefs and activities. Here we must insist upon the distinction between mutual knowledge and common sense. Scientific ideas may derive from common-sense beliefs and concepts, as well as place them in question. Sometimes such beliefs act as stimulants and at other times as constraints upon natural science investigations. The concepts and findings of the natural sciences do not remain separate from the social world, or from interventions, conceptual and technological, which human beings make into the world of nature. The hermeneutics of natural science, and the associated activities of the construction of investigatory procedures, are not confined to the interplay of technical meanings. Since Gödel, we know that even the most formal systems of mathematics presume 'outside' concepts, and obviously ordinary language is the medium by which scientific procedures and discussions are produced and carried on. It is certainly not true that the thesis of the double hermeneutic as specific to social science implies a prohibition upon interactions between science and lay culture.

The relation between the natural scientist and his or her field of investigation, however, is neither constituted nor mediated by mutual knowledge, in the way I have defined that term – unlike the relations between scientists themselves or between them and the lay public. This is why the double hermeneutic has peculiar reference to the social sciences. It is not affected by the fact that, in respect of both natural and social science, some people speak on account of those who remain silent or inarticulate. Nor is the position affected by constructivism, even in its more radical guises. For no one suggests that it is the natural world which constructs accounts of itself.

One consequence of the double hermeneutic is that original ideas and findings in social science tend to 'disappear' to the degree to which they are incorporated within the familiar components of practical activities. This is one of the main reasons why social science does not have parallel 'technological' applications to natural science, and why it typically sustains less prestige in the public eye than the natural sciences do. For the most interesting and challenging ideas are precisely those most likely to be seized upon in lay domains – although, to emphasize the point again, with many differing possible outcomes. Superficially, modern civilization seems almost wholly dominated by natural science; the social sciences are very much the poor relations, which hardly get a look in. In reality, the impact of social science – understood in the widest possible way, as systematic and informed reflection upon the conditions of social activity – is of core significance to modern institutions, which are unthinkable without it.

In revising the text of the book, I have not sought to make major changes. Nor have I added any substantially new sections, but have limited myself to making stylistic alterations and eliminating one or two paragraphs referring to material that has now become excessively dated. I have taken out about half of the notes from the original edition, but have not tried to update those that remain; the bibliography from the first edition has also been omitted.

Introduction to the
First Edition

As we know them today, the social sciences were shaped by the spectacular advances of natural science and technology in the late eighteenth and the nineteenth centuries. I say this bluntly, in awareness of the complexities which it conceals. It would certainly not be true to say that the successes of human beings in seemingly mastering nature intellectually in science, and materially in technology, were adopted uncritically as forming a model for social thought. Throughout the nineteenth century, idealism in social philosophy and romanticism in literature, in their various guises, maintained their distance from the intellectual standpoints fostered by the natural sciences, and normally expressed deep hostility to the spread of machine technology. But for the most part, authors within these traditions were as sceptical of the possibility of creating a science of society as they were distrustful of the claims of the sciences of nature, and their views served as no more than a critical foil to the much more influential writings of those who sought to create just such a science. Mentioning just one or two figures in isolation is risky, but I think it reasonable to regard Comte and Marx as the pre-eminent influences upon the subsequent development of the social sciences (I shall use this term primarily to refer to sociology and anthropology, but shall also on occasion make reference to economics and to history). Comte's influence is fundamental since, as projected through Durkheim's writings, his conception of sociological method can readily be traced through to some of the basic themes of 'academic sociology' and anthropology in the twentieth century. Following Marx's own scornful dismissal of Comte, Marxism set itself against those streams of social theory connected to the emphases of the former author. Comte's formulation of the idea of a natural science of society was actually a sophisticated one, as anyone can check for himself by glancing through no more than a few pages of the *Philosophie Positive*, even if it lacked the subtleties (and, it must be said, some of the logical difficulties) of Marx's work, informed as the latter was by a transposed Hegelian dialectic. Both Comte and Marx wrote in the shadow of the triumphs of natural science, and both regarded the extension of science to the study of human conduct in society as a direct outcome of the progressive march of human understanding towards humanity itself.

Comte sanctified this as a doctrine. The 'hierarchy of the sciences' expresses not only a logical order of relations but an historical one too. Human knowledge first of all dispels the shrouds of mysticism in those areas of nature furthest from human involvement and control, in which humanity appears to play no role as subject: first mathematics, and then astronomy. The development of science subsequently edges closer and closer to human life, moving through physics, chemistry and biology to the creation of sociology, the science of human conduct in society. It is easy to see how, even before Darwin, evolutionary theory in biology seemed to prepare the stage for the explication of human conduct according to principles of scientific reason, and to appreciate Marx's enthusiasm for the *Origin of Species* as offering a parallel to what he and Engels sought to accomplish in their work.

An end to mystery, and an end to mystification: this is what Comte and Marx alike anticipated and strove for. If nature could be revealed as a secular order, why should human social life remain enigmatic? For perhaps there is only a short step from scientific knowledge to technical mastery; with a precise scientific understanding of the conditions of their own social existence, why should not people be able rationally to shape their own destiny? The Marxian vision is ambiguous: and some versions of what Marx had to say, I believe, can be reconciled without difficulty, on the level of ontology at least, with this present study. I refer to those versions of Marx which regard Marxism, not as a natural science of society which happened to predict the demise of capitalism and its replacement by socialism, but as an informed investigation into the historical interconnections of subjectivity and objectivity in human social existence. But in so far as there were strongly naturalistic strains in Marx's writings, and most certainly there were, Marx can be categorized along with Comte as previsaging, and seeking to bring into being, a science of society which would reproduce, in the study of human social life, the same kind of sensational illumination and explanatory power already yielded up by the sciences of nature. By this token, social science must surely be reckoned a failure. Beside the seeming certainties, the system of precise laws attained in classical mechanics, that model for all aspiring sciences after Newton, which in the nineteenth century was unquestioningly assumed to be the goal to be emulated, the achievements of the social sciences do not look impressive.

This much is accepted, and necessarily so, by those in the social sciences today who cling to the same sort of ideal. The wish to establish a natural science of society, which would possess the same sort of logical structure and pursue the same achievements as the sciences of nature, remains prominent. Of course, many who accept it have relinquished the belief, for various reasons, that social science, in the near future, will be able to match the precision or the explanatory scope of even the less advanced natural sciences. However, a sort of yearning for the arrival of a social-scientific Newton remains common enough, even if today there are perhaps many more who are sceptical of such a possibility than still cherish such a hope. But those who still wait for a Newton are not only waiting for a train that will not arrive, they are in the wrong station altogether.

It is of the first importance, of course, to trace out the process whereby the certainties of natural science itself have been assaulted in the twentieth century. This has to a large extent come about through the internal transformation of physics and the setting aside of Newton by Einsteinian relativity, complementarity theory and the 'uncertainty principle'. But of equal significance, to this study at least, is the appearance of new forms of the philosophy of science. One might identify two intertwining yet ultimately opposed trends in the philosophy of science over the past forty or fifty years, in the wake of the perturbations experienced in classical physics. On the one side – and this is not at all paradoxical – there has been the attempt to sustain the claim that natural scientific knowledge, or a particular characterization of it, should be regarded as the exemplar of everything which can be regarded legitimately as 'knowledge'. If the famous 'verification principle' was itself rapidly shown to be incapable of verification, and the radical attempt to expunge metaphysics from human affairs was soon abandoned, the influence of logical positivism or logical empiricism remains strong, if not preponderant. In recent decades, this orthodoxy has been challenged with mounting success. In this challenge the works of Karl Popper played a pivotal, if not entirely unambiguous, role. Whatever Popper's original views may have been, his critique of inductive logic and his insistence that, though claims to knowledge in science have to begin somewhere, there is nowhere where they *have* to begin, were of decisive importance, not only for their own value, but as a springboard for many subsequent contributions.

Some such discussions in natural science have an immediate significance for epistemological problems in the social sciences. But in any case I want to assert that social science should move out of the shadow of the natural sciences, in whatever philosophical mantle the latter be clad. By this I do not mean to say that the logic and method of the study of human social conduct are wholly discrepant with those involved in the study of nature, which I certainly do not believe; nor do I propose to support the view expressed by those in the tradition of the *Geisteswissenschaften*, according to which any sort of generalizing social science is logically ruled out of court. But any approach to the social sciences which seeks to express their epistemology and ambitions as directly similar to those of the sciences of nature is condemned to failure in its own terms, and can only result in a limited understanding of human society.

The failure of social science, when thought of as a natural science of society, is manifest not only in the lack of an integrated corpus of abstract laws, whose circumstances of application are precisely known, and which meet with the acceptance of a 'professional community'; it is evident in the response of the lay public. Conceived as a project by Comte and Marx, social science was to be revelatory, to sweep away the opaque prejudices of earlier times and replace them with rational self-understanding. What appears as the 'resistance' of the lay public to the 'findings' of social science is often simply equated with the opposition that has sometimes been provoked by theories of the natural world: for example, a disinclination to accept that the world is spherical rather than flat. But that sort of resistance is aroused by scientific theories or discoveries which shake or disturb common sense (I do not want to touch here upon the opposition of vested interests to scientific ideas). The objection which lay members of society frequently have to the claims of sociology is just the opposite: that its 'findings' tell them nothing which they did not already know – or worse, dress up in technical language that which is perfectly familiar in everyday terminology. There is a disinclination among those involved in the social sciences to take this sort of protest seriously: after all, haven't the natural sciences often shown that beliefs which people took for granted, which they 'knew', were in fact mistaken? Why should we not merely say that it is the task of social science to check upon common sense, to see whether lay members of society do really know what they claim to know? I want to suggest, however, that we have to take the objection seriously, even if in the end it is not sustained: for, in some sense that is not at all easy to spell out, society is the outcome of the consciously applied skills of human agents.

The difference between society and nature is that nature is not a human product, is not created *by* human action. While not made by any single person, society is created and recreated afresh, if not *ex nihilo*, by the participants in every social encounter. *The production of society* is a skilled performance, sustained and 'made to happen' by human beings. It is indeed only made possible because every (competent) member of society is a practical social theorist; in sustaining any sort of encounter he or she draws upon social knowledge and theories, normally in an unforced and routine way, and the use of these practical resources is precisely the condition of the production of the encounter at all. Such resources (which I shall later call generically 'mutual knowledge') *as such* are not corrigible in the light of the theories of social scientists, but are routinely drawn upon by them in the course of any researches they may prosecute. That is to say, a grasp of the resources used by members of society to generate social interaction is a condition of the social scientist's understanding of their conduct in just the same way as it is for those members themselves. While this is easily appreciated by an anthropologist who visits an alien culture, and who seeks to describe the conduct observed there, it is not as transparent to anyone studying conduct within a familiar cultural frame, who tends to take such mutual knowledge for granted.

Recent developments in sociology, drawing in large part upon not so recent developments in analytic philosophy and phenomenology, have been very much concerned with these matters. That such an interchange between the social sciences and philosophy should have occurred is not surprising, since what distinguishes some of the leading standpoints within these broad philosophical traditions – namely 'existential phenomenology', 'ordinary language philosophy' and the philosophy of the later Wittgenstein – is a resurgent interest in action, meaning and convention in the context of human social life. Now a concern with problems of action is certainly not alien to existing orthodoxies in the social sciences. The term 'action' itself, in the shape of the 'action frame of reference' occupies a prime place in the work of Talcott Parsons. In his earlier writings at least, Parsons specifically sought to incorporate a 'voluntaristic' frame within his approach. But Parsons (like J. S. Mill) went on to identify voluntarism with the 'internalization of values' in personality and hence with psychological motivation ('need-dispositions'). *There is no action in Parsons's 'action frame of reference'*, only behaviour which is propelled by need-dispositions or role-expectations. The stage is set, but the actors only perform according to scripts which have already been written out for them. I shall try to trace out some further implications of this later on in this study. But is it any wonder that laypeople find it hard to recognize themselves in such theories? For although Parsons's writings are in these respects vastly more sophisticated than those of many others, we do not appear in them as skilled and knowledgeable agents, as at least to some extent masters of our own fate.

The first part of this study consists of a brief and critical Cook's tour through some prominent schools of social thought and social philosophy. There are striking, and not very widely acknowledged, points of connection between, on the more abstract level of the philosophy of being, Heidegger and the later Wittgenstein and, so far as the social sciences are concerned, the lesser figures of Schutz and Winch. There is one very substantial difference between the latter two: Schutz's philosophy remained wedded to the standpoint of the ego, and hence to the notion that we can never achieve more than a fragmentary and imperfect knowledge of the other, whose consciousness must forever remain closed to us; while for Winch, following Wittgenstein, even our knowledge of ourselves is achieved through publicly accessible semantic categories. But both insist that, in formulating descriptions of social conduct, the observing social scientist does, and must, depend upon the typifications, in Schutz's term, used by members of society themselves to describe or account for their actions; and each, in his different way, underlines the significance of reflexivity or self-awareness in human conduct. Since what they have to say is in some respects not too dissimilar, it is not very surprising that their writings have much the same sort of limitations – limitations which I think are shared by many who have written about the 'philosophy of action', especially those, like Winch, influenced above all by the later Wittgenstein. 'Post-Wittgensteinian philosophy' plants us firmly in society, emphasizing both the multifold character of language and the way it is embedded in social practices. However, it also leaves us there. The rules governing a form of life are taken as a parameter, within and with reference to which modes of conduct may be 'deciphered' and described. But two things are left obscure: how one is to set about analysing the transformation of forms of life over time; and how the rules governing one form of life are to be connected to, or expressed in terms of, those governing other forms of life. As some of Winch's critics have pointed out (Gellner, Apel, Habermas), this easily terminates in a relativism which breaks off just where some of the basic issues which confront sociology begin: problems of institutional change and the mediation of different cultures.

It is remarkable how frequently conceptions which at least in certain important respects parallel that of 'forms of life' (language-games) appear in schools of philosophy or social theory which have little or no direct connection to Wittgenstein's *Philosophical Investigations*: 'multiple realities' (James, Schutz), 'alternate realities' (Castaneda), 'language structures' (Whorf), 'problematics' (Bachelard, Althusser), 'paradigms' (Kuhn). There are, of course, very basic differences between the philosophical standpoints which these express, and the sorts of problems which their authors have developed to try to illuminate them. Each of them in some part signals a movement along a broad front in modern philosophy away from empiricism and logical atomism in the theory of meaning; but it is not difficult to see how the emphasis upon discrete 'universes of meaning' can allow the principle of *relativity* of meaning and experience to become *relativism* caught in a vicious logical circle, and unable to deal with problems of meaning-variance. I shall try to show in the course of this study how it is possible, and important, to sustain a principle of relativity while rejecting relativism. This depends upon escaping from the tendency of some if not most of the authors just mentioned to treat universes of meaning as 'self-contained' or unmediated. Just as knowledge of the self is, from the earliest experience of the infant, acquired through knowledge of others (as G. H. Mead showed), so the learning of a language-game, the participation in a form of life, occurs in the context of learning about other forms of life that are specifically rejected or are to be distinguished from it. This is surely compatible with Wittgenstein, whatever some of his followers may have made of his ideas: a single 'culture' incorporates many types of language-game on levels of practical activity, ritual, play and art; and to become acquainted with that culture, as a growing infant or as an alien observer or visitor, is to come to grasp the mediations of these in moving between languages of representation, instrumentality, symbolism etc. In quite different contexts, Schutz talks of the 'shock' of moving between different 'realities', and Kuhn refers to the apprehension of a new 'paradigm' as a sudden 'Gestalt switch'. But although such sudden transitions no doubt occur, the ordinary member of society quite routinely shifts between different orders of language and activity, as do scientists on the level of theoretical reflection.

Parsons argued that the most significant convergent idea in modern social thought concerns the 'internalization of values', as independently arrived at by Durkheim and Freud; I think a better case can be made for the notion of the social (and *linguistic*) foundation of reflexivity, as independently arrived at, from widely varying perspectives, by Mead, Wittgenstein and Heidegger – and, following the latter, Gadamer. Self-consciousness has always been regarded, in positivistically inclined schools of social theory, as a nuisance to be minimized; these schools endeavour to substitute external observation for 'introspection'. The specific 'unreliability' of the 'interpretation of consciousness', indeed, whether by the self or by an observer, has always been the principal rationale for the rejection of *Verstehen* by such schools. The intuitive or empathic grasp of consciousness is regarded by them merely as a possible source of *hypotheses* about human conduct (a view which is echoed even in Weber). In the tradition of the *Geisteswissenschaften* in the nineteenth and early twentieth centuries, *Verstehen* was regarded above all as a *method*, a means of studying human activity, and as such as depending upon the 'reliving' or 're-enactment' of the experiences of others. Such a view, as held by Dilthey and later in modified form by Weber, was certainly vulnerable to the strictures levelled against it by positivistic opponents, since both Dilthey and Weber, in their varying ways, wanted to claim that the 'method of understanding' yields material of an 'objective', and therefore intersubjectively verifiable, kind. But what these writers called 'understanding' is not merely a method for making sense of what others do, nor does it require an emphatic grasp of their consciousness in some mysterious or obscure fashion: *it is the very ontological condition of human life in society as such.* This is the central insight of Wittgenstein and of certain versions of existentialist phenomenology; self-understanding is connected integrally to the understanding of others. Intentionality, in the phenomenological sense, is not thus to be treated as an expression of an ineffable inner world of private mental experiences, but as *necessarily* drawing upon the communicative categories of language, which in turn presuppose definite forms of life. Understanding what one does is only made possible by understanding, that is, being able to describe, what others do, and vice versa. It is a semantic matter, rather than a matter of empathy; and reflexivity, as the distinctive property of the human species, is intimately and integrally dependent upon the social character of language.

Language is first of all a symbolic or sign-system; but it is not simply, or even primarily, a structure of 'potential descriptions' – it is a medium of practical social activity. The organization of 'accountability', as has been made fully clear in existentialist phenomenology after Heidegger, is the fundamental condition of social life; the production of 'sense' in communicative acts is, like the production of society which it underpins, a skilled accomplishment of actors – an accomplishment that is taken for granted, yet is only achieved because it is never wholly taken for granted. Meaning in communicative acts, as it is produced by lay actors, cannot be grasped simply in terms of a lexicon, any more than it can be transcribed within frameworks of formal logic that pay no attention to context-dependence. This is surely one of the ironies of some sorts of supposedly precise 'measures' employed in the social sciences, quite properly resented by the lay public since the categories often appear foreign and imposed.

In this study, I discuss several schools of thought in social theory and social philosophy, from the phenomenology of Schutz to recent developments in hermeneutic philosophy and critical theory. I shall try to make it clear what, if anything, I have borrowed from each of these schools, and shall attempt to indicate some of their shortcomings. This essay is not, however, intended to be a work of synthesis, and while I shall specifically draw attention to several parallel currents in social thought in the contemporary period, it is not my objective to seek to show an immanent process of convergence which will finally establish a secure logical framework for sociology. There are some standpoints in contemporary social thought which I have not analysed in a detailed way, even though much of what I have to say bears directly upon them. I have in mind *functionalism*, *structuralism* and *symbolic interactionism* – labels for an array of views which are diverse, to be sure, but each of which possesses certain central and distinctive themes of its own. I shall indicate only cursorily here why the arguments developed in this study diverge from those characteristic of such traditions of social theory.

There are four key respects in which I shall say that functionalism, as represented at least by Durkheim and Parsons, is essentially wanting. One I have already alluded to earlier: the reduction of human agency to the 'internalization of values'. Second: the concomitant failure to treat social life as *actively constituted* through the doings of its members. Third: the treatment of power as a *secondary* phenomenon, with norm or 'value' residing in solitary state as the most basic feature of social activity and consequently of social theory. Fourth: the failure to make conceptually central the *negotiated* character of norms, as open to divergent and conflicting 'interpretations' in relation to divergent and conflicting *interests* in society. The implications of these failures are so damaging, I think, that they undermine any attempt to remedy any rescue functionalism by reconciling it with other perspectives of a different sort.

Use of the term 'structure' has no particular connection with 'structuralism', any more than 'sign' has with semiology. I definitely want to maintain that 'structure' is a necessary concept in social theory and shall make use of it below. But I shall want to distinguish my version of the concept both from that characteristic of Anglo-American functionalism, where 'structure' appears as a 'descriptive' term, and from that of the French structuralists, who use it in a reductive way; both types of usage of the notion of structure, I shall say, lead to the conceptual blotting-out of the active subject.

Symbolic interactionism is the only one of these three schools of thought to accord primacy to the subject as a skilled and creative actor; in American social theory in particular it was for many decades the only major rival to functionalism. Mead's social philosophy, in an important sense, was built around reflexivity: the reciprocity of the 'I' and the 'me'. But even in Mead's own writings, the *constituting* activity of the 'I' is not stressed. Rather, it is the 'social self' with which Mead was preoccupied; and this emphasis has become even more pronounced in the writings of most of his followers. Hence much of the possible impact of this theoretical style has been lost, since the 'social self' can easily be reinterpreted as the 'socially determined self', and from then on the differences between symbolic inter-actionism and functionalism become much less marked. This explains why the two have been able to come together in American social theory, where the differentiation between symbolic interactionism – which from Mead to Goffman has lacked a theory of institutions and institutional change – and functionalism has become typically regarded as merely a division of labour between 'micro-' and 'macro-sociology'. I wish to emphasize in this study, however, that the problem of the relation between the constitution (or, as I shall often say, production and re-production) of society by actors, and the constitution of those actors by the society of which they are members, has nothing to do with a differentiation between micro- and macro-sociology; it cuts across any such division.

1

Some Schools of Social Theory and Philosophy

In this chapter I shall discuss what might initially appear a puzzling diversity of schools of thought. However, they all share some common themes and have certain definite interconnections. All are concerned, in some sense or another, with problems of language and meaning in relation to the 'interpretative understanding' of human action. I shall not be interested in analysing, in any detail, the intellectual sources which tie together the traditions upon which they draw. One can readily distinguish at least three such traditions. The longest-established is that of the *Geisteswissenschaften*, or 'hermeneutic philosophy', which in Germany dates back to the eighteenth century. It is, of course, rich and complex, held together as a distinctive body of thought by the centrality accorded the notion of *Verstehen* in the study of human conduct, and by a continuing emphasis upon a radical differentiation between the problems of the social and the natural sciences. Max Weber was deeply influenced by this tradition, although at the same time highly critical of it. It is largely through his writings that the term *Verstehen* has become familiar coinage among social scientists in the English-speaking world. I shall not evaluate Weber's version of 'interpretative sociology' here because many critical analyses of it are already available in the literature; but also because, as should become clear subsequently, I regard much of Weber's discussion of the interpretation and explanation of action as obsolete in the light of subsequent developments in the philosophy of method.

The second stream of thought – perhaps too recent to be aptly called a 'tradition' – is that deriving from the influence of the later Wittgenstein. Most strongly based in Anglo-Saxon philosophy, this can be broadly grouped together with the 'ordinary language philosophy' of Austin, and its subsequent development. Few authors affiliated to the standpoints of either Wittgenstein or Austin have been at all indebted to continental hermeneutics. None the less, it now seems clear that there are important points of overlap, in respect both of the issues that have come to the fore and the modes of approach to them.

Phenomenology, the third of the schools of thought which figures prominently in this chapter, has in some part served as a broker between the other two. The complicated ramification of connections can be briefly traced through as follows. Schutz's writings draw heavily upon those of Husserl; but Schutz also conjoins Husserl to Weber, and thus is indirectly linked to the tradition of the *Geisteswissenschaften*. The work of Garfinkel in turn takes its point of departure from that of Schutz, and relates the latter to ideas adopted from Wittgenstein and Austin. Wittgenstein's *Philosophical Investigations* is the main stimulus to the writings of Winch: as certain authors mentioned below have indicated, there are evident similarities between Winch's views and those developed by the leading figure in contemporary hermeneutic philosophy, Gadamer. Gadamer's work is itself profoundly influenced by one offshoot of the phenomenological tradition, that represented by Heidegger.

Existential phenomenology: Schutz

It would be fair to say that phenomenology has only recently been discovered by English-speaking authors in the social sciences; at least, it is only over the past two decades or so that the writings of phenomenological philosophers have commanded widespread attention. But Husserl's writings date from about the same period as those of Weber, and Schutz wrote his major work attempting to develop themes from these two thinkers at roughly the same time as Parsons published *The Structure of Social Action*.[1] To speak of 'phenomenology' is not to speak of a single, unified body of thought. Husserl has had various important followers, but few of them have pursued the same paths that he did. Although I shall not spell out the differences between the philosophical approaches of such writers as Scheler, Heidegger, Merleau-Ponty or Sartre, it is as well to remember that the phenomenological tradition is internally a considerably diversified one.

Husserl's prime aim, at least in his earlier writings, was to establish a philosophical scheme that transcends empirical knowledge. All consciousness is 'intentional', in the sense which Brentano gave to that term. This, of course, is not what we ordinarily mean when we speak in English of 'intended' action. Brentano had in mind an idea that he traced back to the Scholastics: that consciousness always has an object that constitutes it. Consequently epistemology implies ontology; knowledge implies being; and the 'objective' (although not the 'real') has no significance except in so far as consciousness is directed upon it. Empiricism, with its central notion of 'sense-data', in a way recognizes this, but is unable to show, Husserl claimed, how thought proceeds from the particular to the general, from specific experiences to abstract classification. An abstract concept cannot be identified with any specific object or event, and is not in any way the sum of a definite number of objects or events. There is an absolute difference between an 'ideal universal' and its concrete 'particulars'. Intentionality involves an 'act of ideation', which is quite distinct from the object of attention itself, and consequently it is this which is the focus of Husserl's interest, since if, in the *epoché*, we 'bracket' all empirical particulars, it seems as if we are able to penetrate to the essence of consciousness. In the quest for a transcendental phenomenology, therefore, the 'lived-in world' and the 'natural attitude' – the ordinary assumptions that we make about the physical world, about other people, and about ourselves, in our day-to-day life – are treated by the early Husserl as just so much bric-à-brac that has to be cleared away in order to reveal subjectivity in its pure form. From this refuge, armed with the means of looking at existence in its most essential aspects, and free from bias, we are then able to re-emerge to conquer the real historical world: we are able to reconstitute it in all its uncouth complexity.

The trouble is that it refuses to be reconstituted. I shall not dwell on this point, because the difficulties which are involved are well known, and indeed stimulated Husserl to revise some of his ideas in his later writings. If we escape from the world into a 'self-contained realm' of consciousness, which has no point of contact with that world whatsoever, what means have we got of philosophically validating its existence at all? Perhaps the 'natural attitude' is not after all merely a screen which we must brush aside in order to penetrate to the essence of things. Certainly in his later works Husserl began to concentrate his attention upon the 'lived-in world', and especially sought to differentiate the 'natural attitude' from that adopted in science, both of which he had previously cast to the winds in the transcendental *epoché*, trying to show that the latter cannot escape from the former in spite of its pretensions to having done so. But it would be wrong to suppose, as some commentators have done, that Husserl radically altered his previous position. His stress upon the 'lived-in world' seemed to have brought him closer to historical actuality, but his attempts at the analysis of it remained on the level of transcendental philosophy: mundane existence was to be constituted phenomenologically. The 'problem' of inter-subjectivity remains intractable; it remains difficult to see how others (indeed, even the concrete self, as opposed to the 'transcendental ego') can be regarded as any more than just another intentional project of consciousness.

The view is very deeply embedded in Western philosophy, since it broke away from hierocratic domination, that the quest for certainty – for knowledge free from presuppositions – is both a necessary task and one which can only be fulfilled through the examination of personal consciousness. Yet the claim that the latter has primacy over other kinds of knowledge, of the 'external' world or of others, has the consequence that a desperate struggle has to be put up to make it possible to accord others anything but a sort of shadowy, epiphenomenal existence. Thus, for Husserl, intentionality is an internal relation of subject and object, and the whole method of phenomenological reduction, whereby the ego, in a grandiose mental act, is able to shed the empirical world, is dependent upon this beginning-point. Husserl developed the notion of intentionality as a reaction against what

he saw as unacceptable premises in previous theories of meaning
and experience, and in doing so he was led to abandon the distinction between sense and reference altogether, in favour of the
meaning-conferring 'ideational act'. Many commentators have
taken issue with this, and have suggested that Husserl's formulation of intentionality should be modified. Thus Ryle comments:

> As it is, if not self-evident, anyhow plausible to say that what I
> know to be the case is so whether I know it or not, a pheno-
> menology operating with this modified notion of intentional-
> ity would not be obviously bound to terminate in an egocentric
> metaphysic, or to claim a priority over all other branches of philo-
> sophy, such as logic or the philosophy of physics.[2]

The question arises, however, whether this would still be a
phenomenology at all, a question which is of more than passing
interest, since most of Husserl's followers relinquished the aim of
producing a transcendental philosophy, and became interested
in human experience in the 'lived-in world': a movement from
essence to existence. In an important way, this punctures the
Husserlian system, and returns it to whence it came, the description of self-experience as outlined by Brentano. But Brentano
was concerned with the psychology of self, rather than the self-
in-the-world which became the preoccupation of Scheler, and
more particularly of Heidegger and Sartre. The strong lean-
ing toward irrationalism, the characteristic outcome of
merging Husserl's scheme with an existentialist one, is particularly
evident in Sartre's early philosophy, the philosophy of the individual alone, in which 'nothingness *haunts* being'.[3] But it is by no
means altogether absent even in the latter's *Critique of Dialectical Reason* and, massive though it is, Sartre hardly makes much
progress towards reconciling the irrationality of human existence
with the irrationality of history, or ontological freedom with
historical necessity.

Of the leading disciples of Husserl, only Schutz began and
ended his career in pursuit of the ambition of applying phenomenological ideas to resolve pre-existing problems of sociology;
and only Schutz continued throughout his life to maintain a
thoroughly rationalist position, according to which phenomenology could and must provide the basis for a fully fledged

science of social conduct. Although Schutz makes his due obeisance to the transcendental ego, his programme is actually completely devoted to a descriptive phenomenology of the lifeworld. Intersubjectivity appears not as a philosophical problem, but as a sociological one (although, I shall claim later, not one that is satisfactorily resolved). Schutz's concerns are with the 'natural attitude' itself, inverting Husserl's *epoché*. The 'natural attitude' does not presume a suspension of belief in material and social reality, but the very opposite; the suspension of doubt that it is anything other than how it appears. This is the *'epoché* of the natural attitude'.[4] In his first and most basic work, Schutz begins from Weber's account of 'meaningful action', seeking to show that while this is in important respects correct, it needs to be complemented and expanded by a study of the natural attitude, or what Schutz also calls variously the 'common-sense world' or the 'everyday world'. Weber's conception of social action, according to Schutz, 'by no means defines a primitive', as he thought it does, but is 'a mere label for a highly complex and ramified area that calls for much further study'.[5] It leaves two questions unanswered: first, what is the sense of Weber's phrase that in action, as contrasted to reflexive 'behaviour', the actor 'attaches a meaning' to what she or he does? Second, in *social* action, how does the actor experience others as separate persons, with their own subjective experiences?

As regards the first of these, Weber is mistaken, Schutz says, in holding that we understand by 'direct observation' the meaning of what a person is doing when carrying out an act such as cutting wood: for to call the activity 'cutting wood' is already to have interpreted it. This is 'objective meaning', which refers to placing observed behaviour within a broad context of interpretation. Moreover, Weber's discussion of meaningful action does not take account of the fact that action is episodic, and from the subjective point of view of the actor has, in Bergson's sense, a duration: it is a 'lived-through' experience. Because Weber fails to give attention to this, he does not see an ambiguity in the notion of action, which can refer either to the subjective experience itself, or to the completed act. It is mistaken to suppose that we 'attach' meaning to action that is being lived through, since we are immersed in the action itself. The 'attaching' of meaning to experiences, which implies a reflexive look at the act by the actor or by others, is something which can only be applied retrospectively, to elapsed acts. Thus it is even misleading to say that experiences are intrinsically meaningful: 'only the already experienced is meaningful, not that which is being experienced'.

The reflexive categorization of acts depends upon identifying the purpose or project which the actor was seeking to obtain: a project, once attained, turns the transitory flow of experience into a completed episode. In this respect, Schutz criticizes Weber for not distinguishing the project of an action – its orientation to a future attainment – from its 'because' motive. Projects, or 'in-order-to' motives, have no explanatory significance in themselves. As Schutz explains this, referring to the action of putting up an umbrella when the weather is wet:

> The project of opening the umbrella is not the cause of that action but only a fancied anticipation. Conversely, the action either 'fulfils' or 'fails to fulfil' the project. In contrast to this situation, the perception of the rain is itself no project of any kind. It does not have any 'connection' with the judgement, 'If I expose myself to the rain, my clothes will get wet; that is not desirable; therefore I must do something to prevent it.' The connection or linkage is brought into being through an intentional [NB: in the phenomenological sense of the term] act of mine whereby I turn to the total complex of my past experience.[6]

The notion of 'relevance' is important in Schutz's writings. In any ongoing course of action, we may discriminate between 'theme' and 'horizon'; the first term refers to those subjectively appraised elements of a situation or action relevant to a particular project which at that time is the actor's concern, while the second refers to aspects of the situation which are disregarded as irrelevant to what he or she seeks to achieve.[7] Life-process, Schutz says, involves constantly shifting systems of relevance according to the interweaving or overlapping of the agent's hierarchy of projects: the flow of lived-through experiences can be analysed in terms of a series of overlapping themes and horizons. Thus a project of finishing reading a novel may be interrupted because one puts down the book to go out to work; the projected act of concluding the novel hence becomes latent or suspended, but remains ready to be reactivated. 'We are involved in the one actual and the many marginal topical relevances with layers of our personality on different levels of depth.'[8]

The understanding of the conduct of others, according to Schutz, can be examined phenomenologically as a process of *typification*, whereby the actor applies learned interpretative schemes to grasp the meanings of what they do. The core social relation is that of the directly experienced other, the 'We-relationship', and all other notions of social forms that are applied by actors in their everyday social life are derived from this. In any face-to-face encounter, the actor brings to the relationship a stock of 'knowledge in hand', or 'common-sense understandings', in terms of which she or he typifies the other and is able to calculate the probable response of the other to her or his actions, and to sustain communication with the other. An actor's 'stock of knowledge' is taken for granted as 'adequate until further notice'; it is 'a totality of "self-evidences" changing from situation to situation, being set into relief at any given time by a background of indeterminacy'. Stocks of knowledge are pragmatic in character. In everyday social action, the agent thus possesses numerous recipes for responding to others, but usually could not, if asked by an observer, explain these as consciously formulated 'theories'.[9] Besides the realm of 'consociates', of We-relationships, however, others also appear in the consciousness of actors as 'contemporaries', whom they hear of or know about, but do not meet directly; and as 'predecessors', the previous generations who lived before they were born. In most of his writings, Schutz concentrates his attention upon We-relationships, since he proposes that it is by analysing these that the significance of the realms of contemporaries and predecessors can be illuminated. There are, he says, no clearly drawn boundaries between these social realms: they shade off into one another. The stocks of knowledge that are applied to make sense of the conduct of others, according to Schutz, constitute and operate within different 'finite provinces of meaning' or 'multiple realities'. It is part of the normal competence of a social actor to shift between such provinces of meaning: to be able to transfer, for example, from the utilitarian world of labour into the realm of the sacred, or into the play-sphere. Such a transfer of attention and response, however, is normally experienced by the actor as a 'shock' – a disjunction between different worlds.

The relevances of lay members of society are geared to the practical tasks of day-to-day social life; those of the sociological observer, on the other hand, are purely 'cognitive' or 'theoretical'.[10] The method of interpretative sociology, according to Schutz, is to establish theoretical constructs of 'typical modes' of conduct so as to illuminate the subjective grounds of action. 'Every social science,' he says, 'including interpretative sociology . . . sets as its primary goal the greatest possible clarification of what is thought about the social world by those living in it.'[11] The concepts formulated in the social sciences obey a 'principle of adequacy'. Such concepts Schutz calls 'second-order' constructs, because they necessarily must relate to the notions actors themselves use in building a meaningful social world. The postulate of adequacy, as Schutz formulates it, states that social-scientific concepts 'must be constructed in such a way that a human act performed within the life-world by an individual actor in the way indicated by the typical construct would be understandable for the actor himself as well as for his fellow-men in terms of common-sense interpretation of everyday life'.[12]

I shall mention later what I take to be the strengths of Schutz's version of existentialist phenomenology; for the moment I propose to concentrate on its shortcomings.

Most of Schutz's discussion of intentionality, time-consciousness and action is based rather directly upon Husserl and, while abandoning Husserl's own epistemological programme, retains the umbilical tie to the subjectivity of the ego which distinguishes the latter's elaboration of transcendental phenomenology. For Schutz the social world is 'strictly speaking, my world': or, as he says in more technical vein, that world 'is essentially only something dependent upon and still within the operating intentionality of an ego-consciousness'.[13] As a consequence, the problems that were engendered by Husserl's intentional consciousness in reconstituting the 'outer world', particularly in respect of intersubjectivity, return to haunt Schutz's phenomenology of the social world. Having adopted the starting-point of a phenomenological reduction, Schutz is unable to reconstitute social reality as an object-world. This emerges plainly in his lame account of 'contemporaries' and 'predecessors', who find a place in Schutz's analyses only in so far as they appear in the consciousness of the actor. Thus 'what at first glance may appear to be a social relationship between myself and one of my predecessors will always turn out to be a case of one-sided other-orientation on my part'.[14] As an example of the rare case in which the behaviour of predecessors may directly influence that of their successors, Schutz is only able to quote the bequeathment of property! But successive generations bequeath far more than this to one another, as Durkheim quite properly emphasized; the social realm cannot be constituted, in the transcendental sense of that term, from the intentional consciousness. That this is so is in fact acknowledged by Schutz himself, who makes no attempt at all to confront the residual problem of intersubjectivity in his exegesis of Husserl's writings. To proceed to the study of the social world, Schutz says, we must 'abandon the strictly phenomenological method': we have here to 'start out by accepting the existence of the social world'.[15]

Unsatisfactory though Weber's account of 'subjectively meaningful action' may have been, he was at least constantly aware of the significance, for sociological analysis, of the 'objective consequences', both intended and unintended, that any given course of action may have for others. No such concern emerges in Schutz's work, the whole orientation of which is towards clarifying the conditions of action, rather than its consequences; and Weber's unremitting emphasis upon differentials of power finds few echoes indeed in what Schutz has to say. Weber stressed, and was entirely right to do so, that social analysis must encompass much more than the 'clarification of what is thought about the social world by those living in it' – both in respect of unacknowledged effects of action and in respect of determining conditions not mediated by the consciousness of the actor.

Schutz's distinction between 'in order to' and 'because' motives is an attempt to rework Weber's differentiation of direct and explanatory understanding. But while Schutz does succeed in revealing some of the inadequacies of Weber's account, his own is not a great deal more satisfactory. Thus 'because' motives are held to cover both the following examples: 'where a man becomes a murderer because of the influence of his companions',[16] and where a person puts up an umbrella because he follows the principle 'If I expose myself unprotected to the rain I will get wet and soon it will become unpleasant. The way to stop this is to open my umbrella, and this is just what I will do.'[17] However, the latter instance refers to an implicit chain of practical reasoning; the former does not, but instead concerns the effects of the conduct of others upon that of the agent. At least one of the implications of this is that, in addition to differentiating between what Schutz calls 'in order to' and 'because' motives, we have to separate out the reflexive application of agents' reasons in enacting specific courses of conduct.

Finally, Schutz's formulation of the 'postulate of adequacy' is unsatisfactory. According to him the terms of a social scientific theory are 'adequate' only if the mode of activity specified by a 'typical construct' would be 'understandable for the actor himself' in terms of the latter's own concepts. But it is not at all clear what this means. If the claim is taken to mean only that sociological concepts, however abstract, must ultimately be matched against concrete forms of meaningful action, this is hardly illuminating. If on the other hand the implication is that the technical concepts of social science must be capable of being translated into ones that can be understood by those to whose conduct they refer, it is difficult to see either why this should be deemed desirable or how it could be accomplished – given that, as Schutz himself points out, the interests, and therefore the criteria, that guide the formulation of sociological concepts are different from those involved in everyday notions.

I do not believe that it is useful to pose such a question as whether there 'can be' or 'cannot be' a phenomenological sociology in an unequivocal way, if only because such a wide spectrum of authors have called their work 'phenomenological', or have explicitly drawn upon Husserl's writings. I do think it correct to say that in Schutz's writings some of the same central difficulties reappear that originally came to the fore in Husserl's transcendental phenomenology, although in an attenuated and altered form. These include the problem of how 'outer' reality is to be constituted phenomenologically, in the sense of either the world of nature or the 'facticity' of social reality; and the so-called 'problem of others' (intersubjectivity), which again is manifest either on the level of the transcendental ego, or on the more mundane level of encompassing and accounting for the existence of collectivities as 'supra-individual' structures.

Ethnomethodology

It could reasonably be argued that phenomenology is a dying philosophy, in spite of the influence of phenomenological notions in sociology. Among Continental philosophers, the post-war flourishing of existentialism – whose success was always something of a *succès de scandale* in any case – tailed off very sharply, interest shifted to other areas, and new perspectives developed. British and American philosophers always kept phenomenology at more than arm's length and, in Britain in particular, the counterpart to 'phenomenological existentialism', with its mixture of complicated technical terminology and blighted moral anxiety, was ordinary language philosophy which displayed all the smug and complacent elegance of the tweedy English country gentleman. 'Ordinary language philosophy', as associated above all with Austin and other post-war Oxford philosophers, and as distinguished from the much broader category which is customarily referred to as 'analytical philosophy', also seems to be today a declining if not a completely spent force. It is therefore rather remarkable that, just as some social scientists have adopted phenomenology, others seem to be in the process of trying to breathe life into another ailing body, in turning their attention to the philosophy of ordinary language. In ethnomethodology we find an attempt to draw upon both of these philosophical standpoints. It is tempting to remark that an endeavour to revive not one but two moribund philosophies, and to combine them together, is hardly likely to produce any worthwhile issue for social science. But this would be unfair: ethnomethodology is a more original and provocative approach than such a description of its parentage would indicate.

For all the differences in style of the two philosophical schools referred to in the previous paragraph, and notwithstanding their almost complete lack of reciprocal influence, it can be plausibly held that they have something in common. Both seem to converge upon the study of the everyday world, the world of the layperson as opposed to that of the scientist. (Austin once, although rather uncomfortably, referred to his work as 'linguistic phenomenology'.) Phenomenology, at least in its non-essentialist guise, insists that the 'natural attitude' is not to be scorned or dismissed in the manner common to most of the older-established philosophical traditions, and particularly evident in positivist philosophies. On the contrary, common sense is a repository of ideas and practices that has to be looked to in order to rebut some of the very mistakes and extravagances of previous philosophers. Here there is also a major point of connection between the philosophies of Austin and Wittgenstein, unifying the general drift of the 'second revolution' in British philosophy.[18]

It seems to have been Schutz's writings, however, that provided the initial stimulus for Garfinkel in the development of his ideas, although the latter has also explicitly acknowledged an indebtedness to Parsons.[19] A good indication of Schutz's influence is found in a relatively early article of Garfinkel's, in which he discusses and tries to amplify the views of that author about the nature of rationality in social conduct. The argument of the paper is based upon a separation which Garfinkel makes between the 'rationality of science' and the rationality of common sense, or of the 'natural attitude'.[20] By the former phrase, he refers to the sort of standpoint that is presumed in Weber's analysis of rational action, involving the application of clearcut means–ends criteria to the explanation of social conduct. From this aspect motivated action is explained in terms of the observer's criteria which may be, and normally are, quite discrepant from those used by actors themselves in orienting their conduct. As a consequence, however, broad areas of human social activity appear to be 'non-rational', and 'rational actions' seem of only marginal significance. If we abandon the idea that there is only one standard of rationality that can be applied to the interpretation of social conduct, and we speak instead of the various 'rationalities' that can be employed by actors, rational action no longer represents merely a residual category. Following Schutz's lead, Garfinkel distinguishes a considerable number of such 'rationalities', which are relevant to the concerns of practical day-to-day life rather than to those of social science. The criteria of rationality that operate in the latter, on the other hand – for example, that concepts should be precisely defined, as generalized as possible, and 'context-free' – are not those which interest lay actors.

The lay actor, as practical social theorist, manages to order her or his experience so as to support the supposition that the world (both natural and social) is as it appears to be – a cryptic formulation that frequently crops up in Garfinkel's writings in some guise or another.

> Out of the set of possible relationships between the actual appearances of the object and the intended object, as for example, a relationship of doubtful correspondence between the two, the person expects that the presupposed undoubted correspondence is the sanctionable one. He expects that the other person employs the same expectancy in a more or less identical fashion, and expects that just as he expects the relationship to hold for the other person the other person expects it to hold for him.[21]

The attitude of the social-scientific observer is the opposite of this, involving the suspension of the belief that things are as they appear, and is (ideally) not influenced by the pragmatic demands that dominate the 'natural attitude'. The two attitudes, that of the scientist and the layperson, do not merge into one another, but are radically discrepant: hence the difficulties that have been encountered in applying the Weberian sort of model of interpretative sociology to the 'understanding' of social action.

Social life, as lived by its actors, is thus to be seen not as a series of feeble attempts to match up to standards of rationality as specified by the 'scientific attitude' but, quite on the contrary, as a series of dazzling performances to which these standards are essentially irrelevant. While the starting-point of this exposition may be Schutz's phenomenology, the result leads in a different direction. Garfinkel has no interest in developing the kind of motive-analysis favoured by the former author, but is concerned with how the 'natural attitude' is *realized* as a phenomenon by actors in day-to-day life. According to Garfinkel, the proposal underlying ethnomethodology 'is that the activities whereby members produce and manage settings of organized everyday affairs are identical with members' procedures for making those settings "accountable" '. Social practices, he says, 'are carried on under the auspices of, and are made to happen as events in, the same ordinary affairs that in organizing they describe'.[22] This leads him away from phenomenology, with its Cartesian emphasis upon the (essential or existential) primacy of subjective experience, towards the study of 'situated actions' as 'publicly' interpreted linguistic forms. It is not hard to see that the direction of movement is towards Austin and towards the later Wittgenstein. For the notion of illocutionary acts, or as Wittgenstein says, that 'the words are also deeds',[23] although serving descriptive rather than philosophical ends, fits fairly closely with Garfinkel's preoccupations.

However, in describing the concerns of ethnomethodology, Garfinkel seeks only rarely to draw upon the terminology of the above-mentioned philosophers, and instead uses the terms 'indexicality' and 'indexical expression', taken from the writings of Bar-Hillel, and ultimately deriving from Peirce. Peirce originally coined the word 'indexical sign' to refer to the fact that a token may have different meanings in different contexts – and that the 'same' semantic components may be expressed by different tokens, according to context (and vice versa). According to Bar-Hillel, more than 90 per cent of the declarative sentence-tokens that a person produces in the course of his or her life are indexical expressions: 'it is plain that most sentences with tensed verbs are indexical, not to mention all those sentences which contain expressions like "I", "you", "here", "there", "now", "yesterday" and "this".'[24] As they occur in ordinary discourse such expressions are the very stuff out of which social activity is organized by its members as a practical accomplishment, Garfinkel claims; but to social-scientific observers, they are just obstructions to the description of social activity. Most formal discussions of method in the social sciences are occupied with 'remedying' indexical expressions, and attempt to rephrase them in such ways as to free them of their indexical character. The use of indexical expressions within routine discourse, however, entails that actors are able to utilize taken-for-granted knowledge in terms of which they are able to locate their sense. This is never something that is given, but depends upon the reflexivity of actors' accounts: the latter are constituent elements of what they are about. Reflexivity is itself taken for granted by social actors of others, and they make use of this knowledge in 'bringing off' any piece of social conduct. 'Members know, require, count on, and make use of this reflexivity to produce, accomplish, recognize, or demonstrate rational-adequacy-for-all-practical-purposes of their procedures and findings.'[25] In any conversation between two or more persons, the 'accountability' of phenomena is a matter of mutual 'work' on the part of the participants: this can be treated as a set of 'glossing practices', whereby 'speakers in the situated particulars of speech mean something different from what they can say in just so many words'.[26]

Such an analysis has clear and important implications for linguistics, where it has been evident for a long time that 'semantics' cannot be handled in terms of the structural properties of language considered as an abstract and self-contained system of 'signs', 'words' or even 'sentences'. This is something which has received a considerable impetus from the writings of Wittgenstein, Austin and Ryle, and the general move away from the emphases epitomized in an earlier generation by Russell's theory of descriptions – and by Carnap's ambitions 'to represent the whole of reality as a universe of logical structures'. Austin's ideas in particular, and at least certain interpretations of the later Wittgenstein, incline towards recommending a descriptive and detailed analysis of the meaning of words in ordinary speech – mainly, of course, in order to resolve, or rather to dissolve, some traditional issues of philosophy. Whatever may be the rights and wrongs of the perennially controversial matter of the proper tasks of philosophy, it makes some sense to propose, as Garfinkel does, that Wittgenstein's later studies can be read as 'examining philosophers' talk as indexical phenomena and ... describing these phenomena without thought of remedy'.[27] There are obvious connections between this comment, as it bears upon the objectives of ethnomethodology as these are defined by Garfinkel, and the work of philosophers of language, who have come to the view that 'the unit of linguistic communication is not, as has generally been supposed, the symbol, word or sentence, or even the token of the symbol, word or sentence, but rather the production or issuance of the symbol, word or sentence in the performance of the speech act.'[28] But most such philosophers and linguists seem still to treat utterances either as the product of abstract individual actors, or alternatively as they relate to equally abstract linguistic rules or conventions, rather than as temporally situated conversations between persons. The significance of the difference, as the studies of Garfinkel, Sacks, Schegloff and others indicate, may be profound. For the meanings conveyed by utterances are brought about in the process of actual conversations, via the mode in which the 'conversational work' is done *in situ*: parts of the conversation are ways in which the conversation itself, and thus also the meaning of its component utterances, is glossed or characterized.

If this definitely suggests that Garfinkel's ideas may be of relevance to linguistics, what of their relationships to problems of sociology? One answer which seems to hold a strong attraction for Garfinkel is that, just as philosophy leaves the world as it is, so ethnomethodology leaves sociology as it is. Thus we are told that: 'Ethnomethodological studies are not directed to formulating or arguing correctives'; that 'although they are directed to the preparation of manuals on sociological methods, these are *in no way* supplements to "standard procedure", but are distinct from them'; and that they do not 'engage in or encourage permissive discussions of theory'.[29] What these statements seem to imply is twofold. First, that the aim of ethnomethodology is to make the accountability of social practices itself accountable, but not to try to 'remedy' indexical expressions in the manner of theories which try to classify and to explain these practices on a general level. Second, that therefore the ethnomethodologist does not differentiate, for the purpose of her or his own studies, between the sociology that lay members of society do in the course of their day-to-day lives, and the sociology that is done by professional social scientists. While the latter have a 'remedial programme' that is much more ambitious than the former, social science is a practical accomplishment like any other rationally accountable form of social activity, and can be studied as such. In case this should simply appear like advocating some sort of sociology of sociology, Garfinkel hastens to add that there are irreconcilable differences of interest

between what he calls 'constructive analysis', or orthodox sociology, and ethnomethodology, seemingly because the latter is to
be confined to the descriptive study of indexical expressions in
all their empirical variety. This attitude is proclaimed as one of
'ethnomethodological indifference'.

Since there are clear differences between the views of
Garfinkel and those of others who have adopted the term,
'ethnomethodology' cannot readily be evaluated as a whole.
However, the attitude of 'ethnomethodological indifference'
upon which some of these writers, including Garfinkel himself,
insist is rarely maintained with the nonchalance that would
seem simple to preserve if there really were the logical gulf that
is claimed to exist between ethnomethodology and sociology.
This is hardly surprising if we remember the part which Schutz's
writings, with their stated project of 'reconstituting' sociology,
played in influencing the development of Garfinkel's ideas. The
latter's writings are actually replete with observations about
'constructive analysis' that hardly show an attitude of insou-
ciance towards it. There is a fairly clear residue of Schutz's
programme, for example, in the observation that the 'familiar
commonsense world of everyday life . . . exercises an odd and
obstinate sovereignty over the sociologists' claims to adequate
explanation'.[30] In any case, I shall want to say that ethnomethodology can no more be indifferent to sociology than sociology can be to it. If this is not readily apparent, it is at least partly
because most of the authors concerned, including Garfinkel,
typically bundle together a whole series of issues which, although
they do sometimes overlap, are logically separable from one
another. These include the problem of 'rationality' in action and
communication; that of the relation between lay technical concepts; and that of 'indexicality'.

I have already indicated how Garfinkel's notion of the
'accountable' character of social practices emerges from his
discussion of rationality, and his rejection of the view that it is
necessary, or even useful, to attempt to analyse correspondences
between actions and norms of rationality as defined by Weber.
The key to the standpoint that Garfinkel seeks to derive from
this conclusion is found in the statement that while 'a model of
rationality is necessary' in social science 'for the task of deciding

a definition of credible knowledge', no such 'model' is needed when 'coming to terms with the affairs of everyday life'.[31] To ethnomethodology, action is to be treated as 'rational' precisely only in so far as it is 'accountable'; the central postulate of ethnomethodology, indeed, is that the activities that produce the settings of everyday life are identical with actors' procedures for making these settings intelligible. But while this may be the prop making the notion of 'ethnomethodological indifference' plausible, the severing of the two overall types of 'rationality' in this way is not really logically defensible. In the first place, certain elements of what Garfinkel calls 'scientific rationalities' are necessary in giving an account of the accountability of actions – that is to say, making their intelligibility intelligible. As I shall argue in some detail later, these elements must be connected to those of lay actors themselves, or the result is a hopeless relativism. This has to be acknowledged, indeed, precisely in order to sustain the wholly valid point – to express what Schutz and Garfinkel have to say in a different terminology – that the mediation of frames of meaning is a hermeneutic task to which the criteria whereby scientific concepts and theories are judged – precision, generality, context-free lexical definition – are normally irrelevant. Second, identifying rationality with 'accountability' cuts off the description of acts and communications from any analysis of purposive or motivated conduct, the strivings of actors to realize definite interests. This explains, I think, the peculiarly disembodied and empty character of the reports of interactions or conversations that appear in the writings of Garfinkel and others influenced by him. The use of expressions such as 'doing' bureaucracy, 'doing' nuclear physics, treating these as 'artful practices', 'practical accomplishments', etc., is thus misleading. 'Doing a social practice' is much more than rendering it accountable, and this is precisely what makes it an *accomplishment*.

In so far as the attitude of 'ethnomethodological indifference' is seriously carried through, nothing can be said at all about the relation between actors' and observers' accounts of action. For Garfinkel, everyone is treated as a 'member', including social scientists; sociology is merely the practical sociological reasoning of sociologists. Now we may agree that the social scientist is in and of the social world that he or she seeks to describe and analyse, in a way which is different from that of the natural scientist. But there is an inherent oddity in Garfinkel's view which shows that he cannot escape confronting issues posed by the relation between actors' and observers' accounts. This is easily demonstrated if it is pointed out that ethnomethodology is itself an artful practice that is made accountable by its practitioners. Hence it would be possible to take an attitude of 'ethnomethodological indifference' towards members-doing-ethnomethodology; and to take an attitude of 'ethnomethodological indifference'. . . . Yonder lies the abyss!

The same difficulty appears in the writings of those who reject the pose of 'ethnomethodological indifference' in favour of an attempt to rectify what are seen as the failures of 'constructive analysis'. The main theme here is that the data in terms of which sociologists build their theories and attempt to verify them depend on prior 'work' that is carried out by lay actors. The investigation of 'fields' of research such as the study of suicide or crime depends upon the common-sense knowledge or 'background expectancies' whereby actors process and define the phenomenon as a phenomenon – as a 'suicide' or a 'criminal act'. The social-scientific observer, according to this view, studies the 'background expectancies' of, say, the officials involved in the police and law-courts in order to attain a 'valid' or 'accurate' designation of the phenomenon. However, the abyss still yawns. For it is assumed that what members *and* researchers label 'data' and 'findings' have to be understood with reference to background expectancies. But the question obviously arises: whose background expectancies? For if those of the observer besides those of the actors are involved, the result is an infinite regress. The background expectancies of the observer, analysing the background expectancies of the actors, would have to be analysed by a second observer, who of course necessarily draws upon background expectancies in doing this, and so on without end. There is no need to labour the point further. The unresolved perplexities in the work of certain of these writers is demonstrated by the untenable character of the conclusions to which they are led: in particular, that social phenomena 'exist' only in so far as lay actors classify or identify them as 'existing'. Once the protective mantle of 'ethnomethodological indifference' is shed, and the assimilation of practical accomplishments with the procedures for making them accountable is turned into an ontological proposition rather than simply a mode of bracketing aspects of the empirical world, such a result seems inevitable.

To be able to extract the elements that are of very real interest and importance in Garfinkel's writings, and in at least some of those influenced by him, the logical circle in which ethno-methodology finds itself has to be subjected to a broader philosophical analysis. It would not of course be accurate to say that either Garfinkel or those who have sought to apply some of what he has to say to the reconstruction of 'orthodox sociology' are unaware of this circularity. On the contrary, they appear to take the view that it can be applied fruitfully. Thus Cicourel says of what he calls 'indefinite triangulation', that 'every procedure that seems to "lock in" evidence, thus to claim a level of adequacy, can itself be subjected to the same sort of analysis that will in turn produce yet another indefinite arrangement of new particulars'.[32] But he does not go on to elucidate in what sense 'evidence' is used here, that is, to develop any philosophical explication of the claim.

In reference to Garfinkel's use of 'indexicality', comparable unresolved issues appear. A famous epigram of Wittgenstein's, *'Ein Ausdruck hat nur im Ströme des Lebens Bedeutung'* ('An expression only has meaning in the flow of life'), might well serve to sum up Garfinkel's direction of interest here. According to him, it is not the task of ethnomethodology to 'repair' indexical expressions.

> Indexical features [he writes] are not particular to laymen's accounts. They are familiar in the accounts of professionals as well. For example, the natural language formula 'The objective reality of social facts is sociology's fundamental principle' is heard by professionals, according to occasion, as a definition of association members' activities, as their slogan, their task, aim, achievement, brag, sales pitch, justification, discovery, social phenomenon, or research constraint.[33]

But this sentence is also necessarily self-referring, as indexical in its own right; and of course the same could be said to be the case of any of the statements about indexical expressions that Garfinkel may make, which themselves must display 'indexical features'.

The difficulty is that indexical expressions, as Garfinkel characterizes them, cannot be redescribed, only 'substituted for'. One should note that 'indexicality', as Garfinkel uses it, is a much more diffuse expression than 'indexical expression' in Bar-Hillel. The latter's point was that many words are dependent for their sense upon aspects of the immediate situation in which they are uttered. Garfinkel elaborates on this from both ends. 'Context' in his usage seems to refer not only to the situation of speech-acts temporally (as ongoing conversations) and physically (as occurring within a definite physical setting, in which aspects of that setting, including facial expressions, etc., are used to formulate meaning). It also seems to refer to the 'contextual location' of utterances within sets of tacit rules. To include the latter with the first two, however, obliterates at least one sense in which 'indexical expressions' may be distinguished from 'context-free' expressions – a distinction that Garfinkel appears to want to retain. For no expression can be 'context-free' in the third sense. The statement '2 × 2 = 4' is only context-free, that is, 'non-indexical', in the first two senses; understanding its meaning certainly presupposes tacitly 'locating' it within knowledge of certain rules of mathematics. Garfinkel's elaboration from the other side of the original connotation of 'indexical expression' involves extending it to comprise what Austin calls the 'illocutionary' and 'perlocutionary' force of utterances – referring to irony, bragging, etc. Now the relation of such performative aspects of locutions to their 'meaning' is a controversial matter. But this, together with the complications indicated above, has at some point to be confronted directly, or else we are stuck with just another voicing of what one philosopher has referred to as 'the wearying platitude that "you can't separate" the meaning of a word from the entire context in which it occurs'.[34] The problems raised by contextual features of action and meaning, however, are certainly not peculiar to ethnomethodology, and are confronted by the other schools of thought I shall now proceed to examine.

Post-Wittgensteinian philosophy: Winch

Consider the following assertion: 'It is a matter of empirical discovery that people talk certain ways, for it is only in the context of the talk that we can claim to understand what they are doing and why they are doing it.'[35] The statement comes, not from an 'ethnomethodologist', but from a philosopher (Louch) in the course of a work that disparagingly attacks the claims of social scientists to be able to construct theories of human conduct that are in any way superior to the explanations that lay actors are capable of giving of their own actions. Explanation of human action, the author argues, is necessarily moral explanation – whether it is attempted by actors themselves, or by 'social-scientific' observers of what they do. When we seek to explain an act, we ask for its 'grounds', which means for the (moral) 'justification' that a person has for doing as he or she does. As soon as we know this, we have no more need to ask why the act occurred. It follows that the social sciences, in so far as they involve trying to go beyond descriptively surveying action, and in lay actors' own language, are just so much verbiage. Anthropology, for example, is, 'a collection of traveller's tales with no particular scientific significance', the same is true of sociology, save that in many cases the tales are familiar, 'and so these accounts seem unnecessary and pretentious'.[36]

The arguments advanced here share affinities with those developed by Winch, although the latter's assessment of the aims and possibilities of social science is more ambiguous than the sweeping judgement which I have just quoted. Winch thinks also that social scientists have pretensions which are doomed to failure, because they mistake the true nature of their endeavours. According to him, the tasks of sociology are essentially philosophical. The claim might initially appear a puzzling one: but we are actually on very familiar ground, for it depends upon the proposal that human action is 'meaningful' in a way in which events in the natural world are not. That which has 'meaning' in this sense, according to Winch, 'is *ipso facto* rule-governed'. Winch is at some pains to demonstrate the universal correspondence between 'meaningful' and 'rule-governed' behaviour.

It might appear at first sight, he says, that only some forms of meaningful conduct are rule-governed. The actions of a bureaucrat involve an orientation to rules, but it is not so easy to see that those of a social rebel, who rejects the norms of the wider society, do so. The point is, Winch holds, that the social rebel still follows a definite way of life, which is oriented to rules no less than that of the strictest conformist. For conduct to be 'rule-governed' it is not necessary, Winch goes on to say, that someone following a rule, if asked, should be able to formulate it consciously; all that matters is 'whether it makes sense to distinguish between a right and a wrong way of doing things in connection with what he does'.

The implications of recognizing that 'meaningful' conduct is necessarily rule-following conduct, according to Winch's analysis, are profound, and show that there is a radical discrepancy between the methods of natural and social science. The 'regularities' which can be discerned in human conduct are not to be explained in the same terms as those that occur in the natural world. Weber was right in emphasizing that human action is usually 'predictable', but wrong in supposing that its explanation can assume a causal form which is logically, if not in content, the same as that characteristic of natural science. A 'regularity' in observed phenomena presupposes criteria of identity, whereby happenings are classified as 'of the same kind'. In social conduct, these criteria are necessarily given by the rules that express different 'forms of life': it is only in this way, for example, that we are able to talk of two actions as 'doing the same thing'.

Natural science, of course, proceeds according to rules; but these govern the activities of the scientist in relation to an independently given subject-matter. In the case of social science, what we study, as well as our procedures for studying it, are activities carried on according to rules, and it is the rules governing the actions that we investigate which supply our criteria of identity, not those involved in our modes of procedure.

So it is quite mistaken in principle to compare the activity of a student of a form of social behaviour with that of, say, an engineer studying the workings of a machine ... If we are going to compare the social student to an engineer, we shall do better to compare him to an apprentice engineer who is studying what engineering – that is, the activity of engineering – is all about. His understanding of social phenomena is more like the engineer's understanding of his colleagues' activities than it is like the engineer's understanding of the mechanical systems he studies.

The study of social conduct necessarily involves 'making sense' of observed actions, and the observer can only do this in terms of the particular rules to which those actions relate. This does not mean, Winch goes on, that the social scientist has to make use of actors' own concepts and nothing more. Technical concepts, however, must always be 'logically tied' (Winch's term) to the former, which have first of all to be 'understood' if the latter are to be applied. Technical redescription does not mean causal explanation. For, Winch says, 'if social relations between men exist only in and through their ideas ... since the relations between ideas are internal relations, social relations must be a species of internal relations too'.[37] This is very simply illustrated by considering the connection between an order given by one person to another and the action of compliance to it. Explaining the act, according to Winch, involves specifying conceptual relations between the notions of 'command' and 'obedience', and is thus quite different from isolating a causal dependency between two events in nature.

Following the first publication of *The Idea of a Social Science*, Winch enlarged upon the views stated there.[38] The issues raised are obviously manifest in their starkest form when we investigate 'forms of life' that are very different from our own. As an example, Winch takes Evans-Pritchard's celebrated analysis of magic and witchcraft among the Azande, phenomena which seem peculiarly alien to those schooled within the context of European culture. We know, Evans-Pritchard assumes, that what the Azande believe about the influence of magic in, say, healing illness, or of witchcraft in producing it, is mistaken. The task, therefore, is to show how magical practices, witchcraft and oracular divination survive in the face of the fact that they do not yield the results which the Azande believe they do. According to Winch, the question is not one that can be legitimately asked in the first place, in the way in which Evans-Pritchard poses it. Magic and witchcraft are central and intrinsic to Zande culture, and thus have to be understood quite differently from similar beliefs and practices in so far as they still linger on in our own culture. It is only within the context of the latter that we can speak of such activities as 'irrational', or even as 'incorrect' or 'mistaken'.

In discussing why we are forced to arrive at this conclusion, Winch quotes Wittgenstein's analysis of games. The rules of a game specify a universe of meaning that pertains within the play-sphere. Now suppose that, in a particular game, a person can always win by means of a simple trick; when the attention of the other players is drawn to this, it ceases to be a game. We cannot say that we have realized that 'it wasn't really a game at all'; the point is that she or he has taught us a *new* game, that is bounded by different principles from the old one. 'We now see something different,' Wittgenstein says, 'and can no longer naïvely go on playing'.[39] In trying to interpret Zande practices in terms of Western ideas of 'scientific understanding', the observer is committing a category-mistake parallel to trying to understand the rules of one game by means of assumptions grounded in the rules of another. The relativistic implications of this sort of analysis are evident; Winch seeks to skirt them by specifying certain constants in relation to which varying cultures may be interpreted. Having rejected 'scientific rationality', he fastens upon what he calls 'limiting notions' which are presupposed by 'the very conception of human life'. These 'limiting notions' – referring to birth, death and sexual relations – 'are inescapably involved in the life of all known human societies in a way which gives us a clue where to look, if we are puzzled about the point of an alien system or institutions'.[40]

The critical reception of Winch's work is by now well developed in the secondary literature, and I shall not attempt to do much more than reformulate some of the chief points made by his critics. First of all, Winch's treatment of 'meaningful action' as equivalent to 'rule-governed' conduct will not do.

1   The notion of 'rule' does too much work in Winch's discussion, and is not adequately explicated. According to him, we

can show whether any given mode of behaviour is rule-governed, and thereby 'meaningful', by reference to whether or not it makes sense to say that there is a 'right' and a 'wrong' way of doing it. But, as MacIntyre asks, is there a right way and wrong way of going for a walk? He concludes that there is not, although we would certainly want to hold that taking an evening stroll is a 'meaningful' activity.[41] In contradistinction to MacIntyre, however, I shall prefer to say that there are actually two senses in which the criterion of doing something 'rightly' or 'wrongly' may be applied to such an activity as going for a walk, and it is a signal failure of Winch's analysis not to distinguish these. One sense is that in which the *linguistic expression* 'going for a walk' might be rightly or wrongly applied to a particular mode of conduct – this would cover the adjudgement of whether being pushed along in a perambulator would correctly be counted as an instance of 'going for a walk'. The second sense refers to *moral* evaluations of right and wrong, and the sanctions associated with them – the sense in which going for a walk down the centre of an arterial highway may be regarded as an infraction of the law.

2   Winch uses 'rule' in a very elastic way, but it is clear that most of what he has to say is informed by a model of linguistic rules or conventions, where conformity is essentially unproblematic. This has two consequences. First, Winch does not once pose the question, *whose* rules? Language, I shall argue later, expresses asymmetries of power; and social norms, especially moral norms, are frequently *imposed* as obligations within systems of domination. Second, there is more than one sort of orientation which actors may develop *vis-à-vis* social norms: knowing the 'meaning' of an action is quite distinct from the commitment to carry it out. Winch does not deal with the sliding scale between moral commitment and cognitive appraisal involved in 'rule-following', which again is directly connected to the significance of power in social life.

3   Thus Winch tends to confuse the meaning of action with its occurrence. According to him there is an 'intrinsic relation' between an act of command and an act of obedience to that command. But this is only so on the level of 'meaning' or the intelligibility of action – what it *means* to use the linguistic

expressions 'command', 'obedience', etc. Rule-following in the sense of the actual occurrence of an act of obedience to a command, as Weber in this respect quite properly emphasized, is not explained by identifying the intelligibility of 'obedience'.

4   Acknowledgement of the latter point undermines Winch's attempt to make a logical case for excluding the possibility of causal analysis from the social sciences, on the basis that actions merely 'express ideas' and the relation between ideas is conceptual rather than causal. It may indeed be correct to hold that the explanation of why someone obeys a command cannot be expressed as an instance of a causal law, but this is a different matter.

5   Winch's account in one rather important respect exaggerates the differences between the social and the natural sciences, because he does not develop the point that 'why-questions' in regard to observations of nature, both lay and professional, are often oriented to problems of intelligibility. Thus a person who asks, 'Why did the sky light up just then?' may accept as an appropriate answer, 'That was sheet-lightning.'

Winch does not wish to argue that the sociological observer, in attempting to explain social conduct, must confine his or her vocabulary to that used by lay actors themselves. But apart from a number of passing comments, no indication is given of the relationship which exists between lay and technical concepts nor, indeed, is it very clear why the latter should be called for at all. Different cultures are so many different 'language-games' that have to be understood in their own terms, and the activities of the social scientist examining this cultural diversity, Winch says, are like using one's knowledge of a language in order to understand a conversation, not like applying scientific generalizations in order to understand how a piece of machinery works. The implications of this view, although they are not spelled out in any detail, belie the author's claim that his analysis simply elucidates what social scientists already do. One of the things which sociologists and anthropologists already do is to try to establish generalizations about different societies that depend upon similarities which are not, and perhaps cannot be, formulated in the terms employed by the members of those societies, because they are directed either towards making comparisons that cannot be expressed in those terms or towards explaining why they exist in the first place. But such endeavours are apparently precluded altogether by Winch's position, which seems to reject outright the possibility of making such comparisons.

That there are logical difficulties inherent in Winch's view is indicated by his scrambled retreat from a full-blown relativism, in speaking of certain 'limiting notions' that exist in all human societies. These turn out to refer to biological universals that in some sense play a part in all human existence, and pose exigencies that have to be adapted to or coped with by any form of social organization. But surely this thesis, although suitably hedged in with qualifications, is precisely of the sort that Winch wishes to adjudge as illegitimate. What we are supposed to do, by reference to such universals, is to elucidate puzzling features of alien institutions: these give us an anchor, as it were, in our attempts to work out the internal relationships within the system of ideas that are 'expressed' in those institutions. However, the ideas relating to the bedrock on which we are supposed to build, one could reply, are themselves imprisoned within the same language-game, and may represent some sort of 'inevitable exigencies' of human existence in ways which have nothing whatever to do with what *we* might regard, from within the form of life of Western culture, as 'biological universals'.

Winch's work was one contribution to a flood of writings by British philosophers from the 1960s onwards, in which the influence of the later Wittgenstein loomed very large, and which were concerned with problems of action and meaning and with explication of these in terms of 'intentions', 'reasons', 'motives', etc. The significance of Winch's work derived perhaps less from its specific originality than from the fact that it was explicitly focused upon the social sciences. The writings of most of those expressing views similar to or overlapping with those of Winch, such as Anscombe, Peters, Melden, Kenny and others, were for the most part notably lacking in any such emphasis. Where they were directed towards any other discipline apart from philosophy, they were concerned with psychology rather than the social sciences (or, perhaps one should say, the other social sciences), and particularly with problems of 'behaviourism'. The impetus behind this concern was undeniably a product of the themes of the *Philosophical Investigations*, with its much-quoted observation that 'in psychology there are experimental methods and *conceptual confusion*'. This relative neglect of the social sciences on the face of it seems rather strange. For it is a major element of 'post-Wittgensteinian philosophy' that, as Winch puts it,

> the philosophical elucidation of human intelligence, and the notions associated with this, require that these notions be placed in the context of the relations between men in society. In so far as there has been a genuine revolution in philosophy in recent years, perhaps it lies in the emphasis on that fact and in the profound working out of its consequences, which we find in Wittgenstein's work.[42]

Ipse dixit. Here lie both the strength and the weakness of the 'philosophical revolution'. Immediately after this statement, Winch quotes Wittgenstein: 'What has to be accepted, the given, is – so one could say – forms of life'. The epigram sums up the new directions of interest in philosophy, and at the same time rigorously circumscribes them. Having discovered social 'convention' or social 'rules', and having perceived that many of the processes of interchange between the individual and the surrounding world are derived from, and expressed in, social conduct, the philosopher takes the forms of social life as given and, as it were, 'works back' from there in attacking problems of philosophy. Established rules set the boundary of investigation, and while the conduct of actors is portrayed as purposeful and cogent, the origins of 'conventions' are left shrouded in mystery, and perhaps even as necessarily inexplicable; they do not appear as 'negotiated', as themselves the product of human action, but rather as the backdrop against which such action becomes intelligible.

Summary: the significance of interpretative sociologies

This is a useful point at which to sum up the contributions and limitations of Schutz's version of phenomenology, ethnomethodology, and the efforts of Winch to apply ideas drawn from the

Philosophical Investigations to problems of sociology. There are rather obvious differences between the three. Schutz's writings stand fairly close to the phenomenological programme originally set out by Husserl; although Schutz abandons transcendental phenomenology, he does so arbitrarily rather than by providing a reasoned case. Hence his work displays an unresolved tension between a phenomenology rooted in the experience of the ego, and a radically different standpoint which begins from the existence of an intersubjective world that is the precondition of self-understanding on the part of the particular subject. In this most basic respect, Schutz's work marks much less of a transformation of phenomenology as inherited from Husserl than that wrought by Heidegger, Gadamer, Ricoeur and others. In their writing, existential phenomenology moves considerably closer to the standpoint independently evolved by the later Wittgenstein, and adopted by Winch, according to which self-understanding is held to be possible only through the appropriation by the subject of publicly available linguistic forms.[43]

Garfinkel draws upon both Schutz and Wittgenstein, not in order to establish a philosophical account of the logic of the social sciences, but to generate a practical series of research studies. Since his main interest is in fostering such studies, the philosophical basis of ethnomethodology remains unelucidated, any development on this level being left to others. In Garfinkel's work, one finds two opposed themes or emphases that are not reconciled with one another. On the one hand, there is a strain towards a quite straightforward naturalism, manifested in the endeavour to provide descriptions, 'free from thought of remedy', of indexical expressions. On the other, there is an acknowledgement of what those in the tradition of the *Geisteswissenschaften* have made familiar as the 'hermeneutic circle': that no description free from 'interpretation' in the light of presuppositions is possible.

However divergent they may be in some respects, the three schools of thought I have discussed above do have a good deal in common. They come together in the following conclusions, each of which I consider to be indeed of profound importance to any assessment of the nature of sociological method. First, *Verstehen* should be treated not as a technique of investigation peculiar to the social scientist, but as generic to all social interaction as such – in Schutz's words – 'the particular experiential form in which commonsense thinking takes cognizance of the social cultural world'.[44] Second, it is the direct implication of this that, in a basic way, social investigators draw upon the same sorts of resources as lay actors do in making sense of the conduct which it is their aim to analyse or explain; and vice versa that the 'practical theorizing' of laypeople cannot merely be dismissed by the observer as an obstacle to the 'scientific' understanding of human conduct, but is a vital element whereby that conduct is *constituted* or 'made to happen' by social actors. Third, the stocks of knowledge routinely drawn upon by members of society to make a meaningful social world depend upon knowledge, largely taken for granted or implicit, of a pragmatically oriented kind: that is to say, 'knowledge' which the agent is rarely able to express in propositional form, and to which the ideals of science – precision of formulation, logical exhaustiveness, clearcut lexical definition, etc. – are not relevant. Fourth, the concepts employed by the social scientist are linked to, or depend upon, a prior understanding of those used by laypeople in sustaining a meaningful social world.

Each of these conclusions demands emendation and further clarification, which I shall seek to provide in the course of this study. The development of such themes in the work of these various authors, moreover, is limited by characteristic weaknesses in their views. First, each deals with action as meaning rather than with action as *Praxis* – the involvement of actors with the practical realization of interests, including the material transformation of nature through human activity. Second, partly as a consequence of the first, none recognizes the centrality of power in social life. Even a transient conversation between two persons is a relation of power, to which the participants may bring unequal resources. The production of an 'orderly' or 'accountable' social world cannot merely be understood as collaborative work carried out by *peers*: meanings that are made to count express asymmetries of power. Third, social norms or rules are capable of differential interpretation; differential interpretation of the 'same' idea-systems lies at the heart of struggles based upon divisions of interest – the struggles between

Catholic and Protestant, for example, that have figured in the history of Western Christianity.

None of the three schools discussed so far has much to offer about problems of institutional transformation and history. It is of some importance, then, to turn to a further tradition which combines a basic interest in such matters with an equal emphasis upon issues of meaning, communication and agency in social life.

Hermeneutics and critical theory: Gadamer, Apel, Habermas

The appropriation of J. S. Mill's term 'moral sciences' by Dilthey was the origin of the concept of the *Geisteswissenschaften*; and yet the latter term today has no direct English equivalent. While adopting a translation of Mill's term, Dilthey none the less sought to question in a profound way the views of the former thinker on the logic and methodology of the sciences of human conduct. The tradition of thought in which Dilthey stands, and in which he was a major formative influence, both antedates the invention of the term that has come to designate it, and contrasts very markedly with the philosophical schools which have dominated in the English-speaking world from Mill onwards. The origins of hermeneutic philosophy in the modern age are perhaps most appropriately attributed to Schleiermacher, but anticipations of Schleiermacher's attempt to found a 'general programme' for hermeneutics can be traced back also to Herder and Friedrich Wolf. While thus part of a tradition of thought which stretches from these authors through Dilthey to Heidegger and Gadamer in more recent German philosophy, the perspectives associated with the *Geisteswissenschaften* have remained largely alien to English-speaking writers, with the exception of one or two philosophers of history (most notably Collingwood). It is therefore particularly interesting to see that some contemporary German philosophers and social thinkers influenced by hermeneutics, such as Apel and Habermas (together with Ricoeur in France), have acknowledged a convergence of thought between contemporary trends in hermeneutic philosophy and the break with logical empiricism signalled in Anglo-

Saxon philosophical writings by 'post-Wittgensteinian' philosophy. Both Apel and Habermas, for example, have explicitly discussed Winch's work; and, while critical of it, they have tried to show that the views developed therein, and more broadly the themes of the *Philosophical Investigations*, independently reach conclusions parallel to those which have become central to hermeneutics.

But this has not come about without a quite major change in the hermeneutic tradition itself, which separates the writings of the more recent authors from their nineteenth-century predecessors. In common with post-Wittgensteinian philosophy, this involves a revised appreciation of the nature of language and its significance in social life; as Gadamer puts it, tersely: '*Verstehen ist sprachgebunden*' ('Understanding is tied to language').[45] The 'early hermeneutics' of Schleiermacher, Dilthey et al. sought to establish the basis of a radical discrepancy between the study of human conduct and the occurrence of events in nature by holding that the former can (and must) be *understood* by grasping the subjective consciousness of that conduct, while the latter can only be causally *explained* 'from the outside'. In the contrast between *Verstehen* ('to understand') and *Erklären* ('to explain') the emphasis is put upon the psychological 're-enactment' (*Nacherleben*) or imaginative reconstruction (*Nachbilden*) of the experience of the other which is demanded of the observer who wishes to study human social life and history.

This sort of conception of *Verstehen*, as set out by Droysen, Dilthey (especially in his earlier writings) and, in a more qualified version, Weber, has been subjected to attack by numerous positivistically minded critics. Most of these critics have held that the method of interpretative understanding may be a useful adjunct to social science, as a source of 'hypotheses' about conduct, but that such hypotheses have to be confirmed by other, less impressionistic descriptions of behaviour. According to Abel, for example, 'the operation of *Verstehen* does two things: it relieves us of a sense of apprehension in connection with behaviour that is unfamiliar or unexpected and it is a source of "hunches", which help us in the formulation of hypotheses'.[46] Given the premises of Dilthey and Weber, it is perhaps hard to resist the force of this sort of criticism, since however much each (Dilthey in particular) wished to insist upon the differences between the study of human beings and the sciences of nature, both wanted to insist that the former are capable of producing results of comparable 'objective validity' to those of the latter. Dilthey's views, in modified form, are not without defenders; but the main thrust of hermeneutic thinking, following the appearance of Gadamer's *Wahrheit und Methode* (1960), has been in a different direction.

Gadamer's version of *Verstehen* emphasizes that understanding such as is involved, for example, in interpreting the actions of people in the past, is not a subjective matter, 'but rather an entering into another tradition, such that past and present constantly mediate each other'.[47] 'Understanding' is still regarded by Gadamer, as it was by Dilthey, as profoundly different from the 'explanation' of events in nature, but Gadamer rejects the notion that this depends upon a psychological 're-enactment' of the experiences of those people the 'meaning' of whose actions is understood; instead it is held to depend upon the interchange between two frames of reference or different cultural frames. What marks off the objects (subjects) whose conduct is studied in the *Geisteswissenschaften* is that, in principle, the observer can, and indeed in a definite sense must, enter into dialogue with them in order to understand how they act. Understanding a text from a historical period remote from the present, for example, or from a culture very different from our own is, according to Gadamer, essentially a creative process in which the observer, through penetrating an alien mode of existence, enriches his or her own self-knowledge through coming to grasp the perspective of others. *Verstehen* consists, not in placing oneself 'inside' the subjective experience of a text's author, but in under-standing literary art through grasping, to use Wittgenstein's term, the 'form of life' which gives it meaning. Understanding is achieved through discourse; *Verstehen* is therefore detached from the Cartesian individualism in which it was grounded by Dilthey (again particularly in his earlier work), and instead related to language as the medium of intersubjectivity and as the concrete expression of 'forms of life', or what Gadamer calls 'traditions'.

In discarding the idea of 'reliving' as central to hermeneutics, Gadamer also abandons the search for 'objective' knowledge in the manner of Dilthey and Weber (although not for 'truth'); all understanding is situated in history, and is understanding from within a particular frame of reference, tradition or culture. According to the notion of the hermeneutic circle, which Gadamer adopts from Heidegger, as the latter puts it, 'Any interpretation which is to contribute understanding, must already have understood what is to be interpreted.'[48] All understanding demands some measure of pre-understanding whereby further understanding is possible. Reading a novel, for instance, involves understanding each particular chapter as one comes to it in terms of a progressively more complete awareness of the overall plot of the book; the comprehension of the global form of the novel, on the other hand, is deepened by grasping particular sequences in it, and this enriched overall understanding in turn helps to produce a fuller appreciation of the specific happenings which are described as the work unfolds. The understanding of human things (works of art, literary texts) via the hermeneutic circle is not, Gadamer says, to be seen as a 'method'. Rather, it is the ontological process of human discourse in operation, in which, through the mediation of language, 'life mediates life'. In Gadamer's words, the understanding of a language 'does not comprise a procedure of interpretation'. To understand a language is to be able to 'live in it' – a principle 'that holds not only for living, but for dead languages'. The hermeneutic problem is therefore not a problem of the accurate mastery of a language, but of the correct understanding of the things that are accomplished (*geschieht*) through the medium of language.[49]

Gadamer's *Wahrheit und Methode* closes with an affirmation of the comprehensive scope of hermeneutics, which is no longer to be confined to the *Geisteswissenschaften*, but extends to all forms of enquiry. There can be no type of enquiry, from the most casual conversation to the apparatus of natural science, that is free from presuppositions, which express the framework of tradition within which alone thought is possible. This does not at all mean, he says, that this framework should be regarded as immune from criticism and revision; on the contrary, whether in day-to-day life, in the literary arts or in the social and natural sciences, it is chronically in a process of transmutation, while all the time remaining the very fabric of our thought and action. Hermeneutics is thus 'a universal mode of philosophy' and 'not merely the methodological foundation of the so-called human sciences'.[50]

The affinities between some main themes of Gadamer's views and those of the later Wittgenstein are striking, since the *Philosophical Investigations*, although written in German, seems uninfluenced by the intellectual sources from which Gadamer draws. If there is one major way in which Wittgenstein's later writing continues the themes of his *Tractatus*, it is in respect of the tenet that the limits of language are the limits of the world; Gadamer echoes this, in saying 'Being is manifest in language.'[51] For Gadamer, as for the later Wittgenstein, language is not first and foremost a system of signs or representations which in some way 'stand for' objects, but an expression of the human mode of 'being in the world'. Apel has sought to show in some detail that these affinities are already apparent in Heidegger. But he indicates, together with Habermas, that Gadamer's philosophy also provides a source of a critical approach to Wittgenstein's work, and more particularly to Winch's endeavour to apply ideas drawn from it to the logic of the social sciences. As Apel remarks, like Dilthey some seven or eight decades before him Winch uses Mill's *Logic* as a polemical foil against which to develop his own views.[52] In doing so, he continues, Winch reaches a position which places him close to hermeneutic theory; but the character of his thought, which is non-historical, prevents him from pursuing its implications fully enough. With his mentor, he stops where the main interests of hermeneutics actually begin, in the contact between different 'forms of life' or 'language-games'. As another commentator has expressed it: 'The difficulties of a language-interpretative sociology according to Winch's model ultimately reveal the boundary of Wittgenstein's philosophy of language itself: it is the boundary beyond which hermeneutics lies and which Wittgenstein did not cross.'[53] According to Apel, Winch's views eventuate in an untenable relativism because he fails to see that there is always a tension, as well as a reciprocity, between three 'moments' of language-games – between the 'use of language', 'practical form of life' and 'understanding of the world'. Thus Western Christianity both forms a unity – a single cultural system – and yet is in constant internal and external dialogue, which is a source of its change over time. The dialogue which is established when two cultures meet is not different in quality from that which is implied within any vital tradition or 'form of life', which is constantly 'transcending itself'.

Habermas has made some considerable use of Gadamer's work in his own writings, which are directed toward connecting hermeneutics with other forms of analysis in the social sciences. While there is a very important sense in which 'interpretation' in the light of (theoretical) presuppositions is necessary to all forms of enquiry, in social or natural science, it is equally important, according to him, to emphasize that the study of human activity cannot be purely hermeneutic – the conclusion which Gadamer and Winch both come to. The thesis of the 'universality of hermeneutics' could only be sustained if human beings were wholly transparent to themselves, in a world of perfect Hegelian rationality. It is necessary, in fact, to resist the 'claim to universality', with regard to the explanation of human conduct, of the two major competing traditions of philosophy: hermeneutics and positivism. Each aspires to cover the whole range of human behaviour, to accommodate it to its particular logical scheme. According to the hermencutic philosophers all human action has to be 'understood', and is refractory to the nomological type of explanation which characterizes the natural sciences; in the eyes of positivistically minded philosophers, on the other hand, the logical form of natural science applies, broadly speaking, in social science also. For Habermas, however, the social sciences are both hermeneutic and nomological ('quasi-naturalistic'); and these two sorts of endeavour have also to be complemented by a third – critical theory.

In his earlier writings, the psychoanalytic encounter, or at least an ideal–typical version of it, was treated as an exemplar of the relations between hermeneutic interpretation, nomological explanation and critical theory: in Habermas's words, as 'the only tangible example of a science incorporating methodical self-reflection'.[54] Psychoanalysis is first and foremost interpretative, since it is the aim of the analyst to understand the verbalizations of the analysand, to explicate their (hidden) meaning – an aim which is accomplished through dialogue. But psychoanalytic theory and practice do not remain at the hermeneutic level; it is an essential objective of psychoanalysis to delve below the descriptions of experience offered by the analysand in order to explain causally why they are distorted representations or conceal material that has become inaccessible to consciousness. In the process of psychoanalytic therapy, the analyst moves constantly from one level, or frame of reference, to the other, thus 'explaining' what lies behind the distorted self-understanding of the individual. In Freud's original writings, this necessary 'tacking' between the hermeneutic and the nomological was not explicitly recognized as such: hence the confusion of terms such as 'energy', used on analogy with physical forces, with those ('symbol', etc.) which refer to 'meaningful' categories. What ties together and yet also balances the hermeneutic and nomological moments of the psychoanalytic encounter, Habermas says, is the emancipatory impulse which is its stimulus. If successful, psychoanalytic therapy translates unconscious processes, which cause the person to behave in ways not subject to his or her own voluntary control, into conscious modes of action which are subject to his or her rational mastery. Psychoanalysis has the critical task, through furthering self-knowledge, of liberating the person from the push and pull of factors which drive his or her activity without the mediation of consciousness.

In Habermas's earlier work, the division of the social sciences into the empirical-analytic (nomological), hermeneutic and critical is integrated with a series of further classifications which connect the epistemology of the social sciences with their concrete subject-matter. The threefold separation just mentioned corresponds to three sorts of 'cognitive interest' which concern human beings in their relation to the social and the natural worlds. Nomological knowledge is directed primarily to an interest in technical control, or technical mastery of a set of causal relations. (This sort of knowledge, Habermas says, is never 'neutral', and it is precisely the tendency, expressed from one aspect in positivistic philosophies, to regard it as the prototype of all knowledge which creates a masked form of legitimation of structures of domination – this is one theme which connects his writing to that of the 'older generation' of Frankfurt philosophers, and beyond them to Lukács.) Hermeneutics, on the other hand, is directed to understanding the participation of actors in an intersubjective 'form of life' and hence to an interest in improving human communication or self-understanding. Critical theory is tied to an 'emancipatory interest' because it seeks to transcend each of the former other types of interest considered separately, by seeking to free individuals from domination: not only from the domination of others, but from their domination by forces which they do not understand or control (including forces that are in fact themselves humanly created).

These three sets of 'knowledge-constitutive' interest are further connected, in the social sciences, to some major substantive conceptual distinctions made by Habermas. One concern of social analysis has to be with *purposive-rational action* (Weber's *Zweckrationalität*), which Habermas also simply labels 'work' or 'labour', and which refers to 'either instrumental action or rational choice or their conjunction'. Instrumental action depends upon nomological knowledge, formed through empirical observation or experience; such knowledge also informs technical decisions about strategies of rational choice. Purposive-rational action has to be conceptually distinguished from 'interaction', which refers to intersubjective communication and symbolism governed by consensual norms (or, in Winch's terms, 'rules'), and is expressed in terms of ordinary language. The meanings-in-context which characterize everyday interaction have to be grasped hermeneutically, by the social-scientific observer as by participants. But the former can make use – as the latter do as a matter of course – of the reflexive character of speech: the fact that ordinary language is its own metalanguage. To the notions of 'work' and 'interaction' one can add that of the assessment of human conduct in the light of encompassing standards of reason, as specified by the tasks of critical theory. Such standards of rationality certainly have to be distinguished from the technical form of purposive-rationality, but they are, for Habermas, as much located 'in history' as is the latter. The progress of human self-understanding moves toward freeing individuals from bondage to causality (in which their behaviour appears as just another series of events 'in nature') by expanding the scope of 'free action'.

In its emphasis upon the centrality of language, and especially of dialogue within and between 'speech communities', Gadamer's philosophy undoubtedly brings hermeneutics closer to other mainstream schools of modern philosophy. We may concur in this respect with Ricoeur when he remarks: 'Language is the common meeting-ground of Wittgenstein's investigations, the English linguistic philosophy, the phenomenology that stems from Husserl, Heidegger's investigations, the works of the Bultmannian school and of the other schools of New Testament exegesis, the works of comparative history, of religion and of anthropology concerning myth, ritual and belief – and finally, psychoanalysis'.[55] Gadamer's account distances his views from those in the earlier tradition of the *Geisteswissenschaften* in so far as, in emphasizing the 'available' character of meaning through shared linguistic expressions, he is able to abandon the 'methodological individualism' of the early Dilthey (and of Weber). There is moreover undoubtedly a coming together – not fully explored – between hermeneutics and the critique of classical empiricism originating in the philosophy of science, in so far as both seek to reject philosophies concerned with 'starting-points'. Ricoeur again puts this aptly when he speaks of the necessity of finding a 'third way' in philosophy as part of his critique of transcendental phenomenology. Transcendental phenomenology disposed of one illusion in philosophy, namely that of objectivism, in which the self is 'lost and forgotten in the world'; but Husserl substituted for this a second illusion, that of the reflexive revelation of the subject.

If Gadamer's writings successfully avoid some of the difficulties of the earlier phase of hermeneutic philosophy, however, they also create others. Certain of these have already been fairly exhaustively examined by Habermas. A purely hermeneutic account of the social sciences places out of court the possibility – which is actually a necessity – of analysing social conduct in terms which go beyond those of actors situated in particular traditions, and which are of explanatory significance in relation to them. Equally important, however, are the problems raised by the model of dialogue itself, as Gadamer elaborates it. Gadamer argues that hermeneutics is 'a discipline which guarantees truth'.[56] But this means that truth inheres in being, the fundamental error of existentialist phenomenology, and one not rescued by Gadamer's appeal to dialectics. Betti has commented that, while Gadamer's exposition of hermeneutics might very well guarantee the internal unity of interpretative materials of, say, a work of literature or of the actions of individuals in another historical period or alien culture, it eschews as non-problematic any further question of the 'correctness' of such interpretations. According to Betti there are four premises of hermeneutics, of which Gadamer only treats the first three: the object has to be understood in its own terms, that is, as a subject ('hermeneutic autonomy'); it has to be understood in context ('meaningful coherence'); and it has to conform to what Betti calls the 'actuality' of the experience of the interpreter ('pre-understanding'). But there is also a fourth element involved which, although it underpins the other three, does not appear in Gadamer's work. This is that of 'meaning-equivalence' (*Sinnadäquanz des Verstehens*): that the interpretation of a human product or action is 'adequate' in relation to the intentions of its originator.

Betti is not alone in offering this sort of criticism of Gadamer's views, and I shall amplify it here. According to Gadamer, hermeneutics is not a method, and it cannot generate accounts that can be adjudged as 'correct' or 'incorrect' in terms of 'what an author meant to communicate' through a text. The meaning of a text does not reside in the communicative intent of its creator, but in the mediation that is established between the work and those who 'understand' it from the context of a different tradition. For Gadamer, following Heidegger, 'language speaks its own meaning': as one of Heidegger's cryptic illuminations has it, *'Ihr Sprechen spricht für uns im Gesprochenen'* ('The speech of others speaks for us in what is spoken'). A written text is thus distinctively different from speech, which presupposes both a speaking subject and another to whom the words are addressed. A work of literary art is meaningful in and of itself, and assumes the 'autonomous being' of language as such. The circumstance of being written down is basic to the hermeneutic phenomenon: a text gains an existence of its own, detached from that of its author.

Since the understanding of a text is a creative mediation of traditions, such understanding is an unending process; it can never be 'completed', because new meanings are continually brought into being through readings of the work within fresh traditions. The attractiveness of the emphasis is evident. Treating understanding as a productive activity, which is not bound by any criteria of interpretative accuracy concerning a writer's intentions in his or her work, seems readily to deal with, say, the numerous different 'readings' of Marx that have been made over the generations since the late nineteenth century. But the difficulty confronting the view is equally obvious: the adoption of one reading, rather than another, appears as an arbitrary matter. Scholarly debates over the analysis of Marx's writings, to pursue the same illustration, seem then to be just wasted effort.

Gadamer is anxious to avoid this kind of 'nihilism': for him, 'truth' exists in the fruitfulness of self-clarification whereby the mutuality of traditions is explored, and an appeal to conformity with tradition serves to help rule out alternative readings among those operating from within it. But this conception is not able to deal with comparisons of readings made from different traditions; nor indeed can one see how it can cope with differing versions of the *same* 'tradition' applied to the understanding of texts, since it seems to presume that traditions are internally unified and coherent (as Winch does 'forms of life'). In the light of all this it is important to follow Betti in stressing the need for recognizing the autonomy of the object – the text as a situated creation of its author – without renouncing the importance of what Gadamer has to say. There is a difference between attempting to understand what an author meant by what she or he wrote and how the text was received among contemporaries to whom it was addressed, on the one hand, and understanding the significance of the text to our own present-day circumstances, on the other.

Recognition of such a difference reinstates hermeneutics as method. Gadamer holds that 'understanding' should not be confused with 'interpretation'. Reading a novel does not demand a process of interpretation; the novel absorbs the reader in a prereflective way. In disclaiming 'method', Gadamer's discussion of hermeneutics, although itself steeped rather heavily in the anti-scientism of Heidegger, bears some affinities with certain perspectives in the philosophy of science – notably Feyerabend's call to 'abandon method'. The importance of these ideas, however, lies not in the disclaiming of method altogether, but in their implications for its reconstruction. Hermeneutics, I wish to claim, does not find its central range of problems in the understanding of written texts as such, but in the mediation of frames of meaning in general. Moreover, there are two orders of hermeneutic problem, whose connection it is vital to trace out, and which span both the social and the natural sciences. One concerns the pre-reflective character of experience, whether in the form of the 'pre-interpreted' character of social reality, or in the form of the 'theory-impregnated' character of observations within the natural sciences (which are not of course wholly discrete). In this sense it is quite right to emphasize that reading a novel, or talking to a chance acquaintance in the street, are not 'interpretative' activities, but are integral to the 'stream of life' which they themselves constitute; the presuppositions in terms of which such activities are 'made sense of' are drawn on in a tacit manner. However, even the daily interchanges of everyday life are not wholly pre-reflective, and (as is made clear in ethnomethodology) the reflexive application of 'accounting procedures' is quite crucial to their continuity: competent social actors in such a respect have shared methods of social interpretation, and the term 'ethnomethodology' is quite aptly applied. 'Method' is hence not peculiar to the social and natural sciences as such, although it is essential to them, and although the criteria of evaluation of 'findings' in the latter are in part discrepant from the accounting procedures of everyday life.

There is an important and instructive contrast between textual hermeneutics, as represented by Gadamer, and the analyses of meaning by recent Anglo-Saxon philosophers. Whereas Gadamer seeks to marginalize actors' intentions in the understanding of texts, some English-speaking philosophers have attempted to explicate 'meaning' directly in terms of intentions (below, pp. 78ff). Perhaps significantly, few such philosophers have been at all concerned with what is involved in understanding written texts. I shall claim later that 'intentionalist' theories of meaning are, as they stand, as untenable as their converse in hermeneutic phenomenology, that 'language speaks'. To over-simplify: if one is close to 'subjective idealism', the other approaches 'objective idealism'. The first is closely linked to subjectivist accounts of action as well as meaning – although not where it is derived directly from Wittgenstein's influence.

Gadamer relies heavily upon Heidegger in supposing that 'what an author meant to communicate' cannot be recaptured, as there is an ontological gulf between present and past; being is in time, and temporal distance is a differentiation of being. Although in accentuating the mediation of traditions through dialogue Gadamer arguably goes beyond the confines of Witt-genstein's discussion of language-games, his standpoint seems in certain key respects to reproduce a Wittgensteinian paralysis of the critical impulse. The distancing of traditions, and the consequent ineffability of that which has passed, foreclose the possibility of subjecting them to critique. This is what Habermas fastens upon.

It is not my aim to offer any sort of comprehensive analysis of Habermas's formulation of critical theory in his later work, and I shall deal only with a few aspects of his notion of 'communicative competence' – mainly in relation to what he calls 'normal' rather than 'distorted' communication. The idea of communicative competence is suggested as a parallel to, yet distinct from, Chomsky's concept of 'linguistic competence'. Chomsky's version is 'monologic', and only leads us to the margins of communication, as an intersubjective phenomenon, which it cannot adequately elucidate; semantic units, or 'meanings', are not merely abstract features of the linguistic equipment of individual persons, but are intersubjectively produced in interaction or *dialogue*. To generate meanings in interaction speakers have not only to be 'competent' in Chomsky's sense (monological) but have to command the social *settings* which turn the mastery of language into the understandings of others: 'producing a situation of potential ordinary language communication belongs by itself to the general competence of the ideal speaker.'[57]

Habermas distinguishes two general features of ordinary language which are basic to communicative competence: first, following Austin, command of the wide-ranging variety of performatives which characterize speech situations as 'promising', 'announcing', 'entreating', etc.; and second, deictic elements (that is, indexical expressions in Bar-Hillel's sense) such as 'I', 'you', 'here', etc., which characterize relations between speakers, or their relation to the 'situation' of communication. Mastery of these can be expressed as a series of dialogue-constituting 'universals': that is, universal features of speech situations which make possible mutuality of understanding in communication. Such universals include:

1   Personal pronouns and their derivatives, which provide a reference system in interaction. These involve above all mastery of the reflexivity of 'I' and 'you': I am 'I' to you, but recognize that you are also 'I' to you while being simultaneously 'you' to me.
2   Deictic terms of time, space and substance – used to constitute a denotive reference system, and thus situate the discourse.
3   Terminologies of address, greeting, question, answer or indirect 'reported speech': all of these are performatives which metalinguistically characterize the act of speech as such (in Garfinkel's words, 'organize the settings whose very features they describe').
4   'Existential' terms, differentiating modes of being. These are expressions which, in appearing as constitutive features of speech situations, characterize them as presuming distinctions between essence and appearance (this work is done by 'conceding', 'showing', 'betraying', etc.), between being and appearance (the differentiation between subjective and public worlds: 'claiming', 'assuring', 'doubting', etc.) and between being and obligation ('obey', 'refuse', 'warn', etc.).

In 'pure dialogue', Habermas proposes – that is, abstracting from the non-linguistic elements in the context of speech acts which always occur in any actual circumstances of communication – we can set up a model of perfect mutual comprehension. This exists where there is complete symmetry between participants, so that 'communication will not be hindered by constraints not arising from its own structure'. Such

a symmetry has three main features: the attainment of 'unre-
strained consensus', reached solely through the rational examination of arguments; the full and mutual understanding of the
other; and the mutual recognition of the authentic right of the
other to take the role she or he does in the dialogue as a full and
equal partner. This leads Habermas back to a concern with
'truth' in norms of communicative interaction. Truth, Habermas
says, drawing in part upon an argument of Strawson's, is not to
be looked for in what guarantees the 'objectivity' of experience,
but 'in the possibility of argumentative corroboration of a truth
claim'. [58] Since 'truth' depends upon rational discourse, for
Habermas, it connects directly with the assessment of communication as 'non-neurotic' (on the level of the person) and 'non-
ideological' (on the level of the group). Truth is not a property
of statements, but of argumentation in a presumed ideal speech
situation.

Habermas's writings from some aspects subsume much of
what is of interest in the schools of thought I have discussed
earlier, drawing freely upon both existentialist phenomenology
and post-Wittgensteinian philosophy, but with a clear awareness
that their scope is limited. None the less, what Habermas provides does not serve as an adequate framework of analysis for
the problems I wish to discuss in this study. This is in some
measure because the principal aim of his writing, that of
elucidating a framework for critical theory in the tradition of
Frankfurt social philosophy, cuts across the themes I want to
pursue; but it is also because of what I take to be quite basic
difficulties in his views. Let me state my objections as follows.

First, Habermas is quite right to suggest that the social
sciences fuse hermeneutic and nomological endeavours, but
tends to operate with too simple a model of the natural sciences,
which are described in a traditional – even positivistic – way.
Habermas in fact rarely discusses the natural sciences directly,
referring to them mainly in relation to the form of knowledge-
claim or 'cognitive interest', in technical control, associated with
them (but also associated with other disciplines). It is important
to emphasize that there *is* a universality to hermeneutics:
scientific theories constitute frames of meaning just as other
'language- games' do. 'Explanation' in the natural sciences

assumes various forms just as in other spheres of enquiry. 'Why-questions' in natural science are certainly not always oriented to general laws, nor do answers to them necessarily involve any reference to such laws: as in regard to human action, to 'understand' – that is, to render 'intelligible' within a frame of meaning – is often to 'explain', that is, to offer an account which 'adequately' resolves a puzzle (cf. below, pp. 155ff).

Second, Habermas appears to follow most post-Wittgensteinian philosophers in assimilating 'meaning' to the interpretation of intentional action, so that the characterization or identification of acts logically depends upon the identification of the purposes for which they were undertaken. But this leads to all sorts of logical and sociological troubles and, as I shall try to show in detail later, is one element uniting approaches to social theory that are nominally opposed to one another: for example, those of Winch and Parsons. Third, Habermas's differentiation between 'work' (labour) and 'interaction' hovers ambiguously across the borderlines of philosophical anthropology and sociology. The distinction appears to derive from the abstract opposition of 'interest in technical control' and 'interest in understanding'. But the logical symmetry of the scheme on this plane tends to defeat its possible application on the more mundane level of social analysis. According to Habermas, 'work' and 'interaction . . . follow rationally reconstructible patterns which are logically independent of one another'.[59] While such a severing of instrumental reason from mutual understanding might be defensible in relation to the logic of divergent claims to knowledge, this is certainly not so in relation to the analysis of social conduct itself. However it be defined, in the encompassing sense of *Praxis* or the more narrow sense of the transformation of nature by human activity, labour is not (except perhaps in a state of alienation) infused solely by instrumental reason; nor is interaction oriented merely to mutual understanding or 'consensus', but to the realization of ends which not infrequently are exclusive of one another. The weaknesses of Habermas's position here seem to be reflected in his critical theory, which, built around the model of a symmetrical 'idealized dialogue', appears to take as its central theme the realization of consensus arrived at through rational debate; but how this relates to circumstances in which struggles, or exploitative domination, are oriented to the distribution of *scarce resources* is not made clear.

Fourth, Habermas's appeal to psychoanalysis as an exemplar of theory and practice for the social sciences as a whole has a definite attractiveness, because it seems to embody each of the features to which he draws attention: the mediation of 'interpretation' by 'explanation', involving the aim of furthering the rational autonomy of the analysand through dialogue with the analyst. Yet there are obvious difficulties with this, which Habermas has acknowledged.[60] Psychoanalysis seems a rather poor model for critical theory, since the relation between analyst and patient is after all a markedly skewed and even authoritarian one; once more, however, Habermas uses only an 'idealized' version of it. More relevant here is that psychoanalytic therapy is an encounter between *individual persons*, entered into voluntarily, in which hermeneutic and nomological analysis appear only in the form of uncovering hidden *motives*. Important as this may be, it give us little clue as to how to connect the explication of human action with the structural properties of social institutions.

I do not want to claim that the discussion offered in the preceding sections is exhaustive: I wish to use it only as a backdrop against which to develop the format of the rest of this study. Among the important issues raised by the various traditions or schools of thought I have examined, but not adequately resolved by any one of them, are the following: problems of agency and the characterization of action; problems of communication and hermeneutic analysis; problems of the explanation of action within the framework of sociological method. The remainder of the book is concerned with their further explication.

2

Agency, Act-identifications and Communicative Intent

A great deal of writing by British and American philosophers, often strongly influenced by the work of the later Wittgenstein even where critical of it, has been concerned with the 'philosophy of action'. In spite of the voluminous character of this literature, its yield has been rather slight. As treated by Anglo-American authors, the 'philosophy of action' mostly shares the limitations of post-Wittgensteinian philosophy as a whole, even where the writers in question are not close disciples of Wittgenstein and substantially diverge from at least certain of his views: in particular a lack of concern with social structure, with institutional development and change. This gap is more than a legitimate division of labour between philosophers and social scientists; it is a weakness that rifts deep into philosophical analyses of the character of human agency. A more immediate reason, however, for the confusing nature of the recent literature in the philosophy of action is a failure to separate out various issues which need clearly to be distinguished from one another. These are: the formulation of *the concept of action or agency*; the connections between the concept of action and that of *intention or purpose*; the *characterization (identification) of types of act*; the significance of *reasons and motives* in relation to agency; and the nature of *communicative acts*.

Problems of agency

It is clear that laypeople, in the course of their day-to-day lives, constantly refer to, or make use of, notions of agency in some way or another – although it is important to emphasize that only in certain instances or contexts (for example, in courts of law) are they likely to be able to give, or be interested in giving, accounts of why or how they do so in abstract terms. People regularly decide about 'responsibility' for outcomes, and monitor their conduct accordingly, as well as basing their responses upon accounts/justifications/excuses offered by others. A different assessment of, and reaction to, a person's conduct is deemed appropriate where someone 'couldn't help' what happened from where he or she 'could help' it. A person who falls ill, for example, may successfully make claims upon others for unusual solicitude, and take time off from ordinary duties. Falling ill is recognized as something which cannot be helped (in Western culture at least, although not universally). But different responses are appropriate if the individual is adjudged to be 'not really ill', or merely 'feigning' illness in order to receive the sympathy of others or to escape from rightful responsibilities. That the boundary line between these is not clear-cut is shown by the ambiguous character of hypochondria, which may be regarded by some as something a person can help, and by others as something for which she or he is not to be held responsible. In so far as they regard 'hypochondria' as a medical syndrome, doctors may of course draw different dividing lines from those accepted by others. Such ambiguities or blurrings between conduct for which agents are deemed responsible, and hence as potentially open to being asked for justifications, and that recognized as 'out of their hands' sustain various forms of manoeuvre or deceit whereby people either seek to escape sanctions upon what they do, or conversely claim a particular outcome as an accomplishment of their own.

In legal theory, a person may be treated as responsible for an act, even though that individual did not realize what he or she was doing or mean to contravene any law. The person is regarded as culpable if it is adjudged that he or she 'should have known', as a citizen, that what he or she did was illegal. Of course, it may happen that the person's ignorance allows him or her to escape sanction altogether, or procures a reduction in the individual punishment (where, for instance, he or she is held not to be in a position to know 'what any competent person should know' – if he or she is diagnosed as 'mentally ill', or, rather more uncertainly, is a visitor to the country, and cannot be expected to be familiar with its laws). In this respect, legal theory represents a formalization of everyday practice, where avowals that one is ignorant of a given consequence of one's doings will not necessarily allow escape from moral sanction: there are certain things that everyone is 'expected to know', or that everyone in a certain category of persons is 'expected to know'. One may be blamed for something one did unintentionally. In day-to-day life, we tend to follow the equation: 'agency' = 'moral responsibility' = 'context of moral justification'. It is easy to see, therefore, why some philosophers have supposed that the concept of agency must be defined in terms of that of moral justification, and hence of moral norms alone.

More commonly, however, philosophers have appealed to a more embracing notion of convention or rule, in seeking to distinguish 'actions' from 'movements'. Peters, for example, quotes the case of signing a contract. This, he says, is an instance of an action because it presupposes the existence of social norms; there is a logical gulf between such statements as 'she sealed the bargain', and 'her hand closed about the hand of another', since the first, describing an action, is framed in relation to a norm, whereas the second is not.[1] But this is not at all convincing. For in endeavouring to specify what agency is, we are presumably interested in differentiating not only statements which refer in some way to the actualization of a norm, like 'she signed the contract', but also ones like 'she wrote with the pen', from ones like 'her hand made movements across the paper'.

A theme of many philosophical writings is that 'movements' can, under certain circumstances – usually those of their connection to particular conventions or rules – 'count' or be 'redescribed' as actions; and, vice versa, that any action can be 'redescribed' as a movement or series of movements (save perhaps for actions which have the character of refraining). This implies that there are two alternative modes or languages of description in terms of which the same conduct may be referred to. Certain readings of Wittgenstein's 'what is left over?' between his raising of his arm and his arm going up readily sanctify this sort of conclusion. But it is an erroneous view if it is taken to mean that there are two alternative, *and equally correct*, modes of describing behaviour. For to refer to an act as a 'movement' is to imply that it is mechanical, something that 'happens to' someone; and it is simply mistaken to describe a piece of behaviour in this way if it is something that someone 'makes happen', or *does*. One can see from this, I think, that we would do well to drop the contrast between actions and movements altogether: the proper unit of reference for an analysis of action has to be the *person*, the *acting self*. There is a further matter related to this. If we use the terminology of 'movements' we tend to suppose that descriptions couched in such a form represent an observation language in a way in which 'action descriptions' do not. That is to say, we tend to presume that, while movements can be directly observed and described, descriptions of actions involve further processes, inference or 'interpretation' (for example, 'interpreting the movement in the light of a rule'). But there really is no basis for such a presumption. We surely observe actions just as immediately as we observe ('involuntary') movements; each equally involves 'interpretation', if this is taken to mean that descriptions of what is observed have to be couched in expressions which presuppose (divergent) theoretical terms.

An extraordinarily large number of philosophers have supposed that the concept of action is essentially centred upon that of intention: that it must refer to 'purposive behaviour'. Such a presumption appears in two guises: (1) in regard of the concept of action generically; (2) in regard of the characterization of *types of act*. But neither view withstands scrutiny. As far as (1) is concerned, it is enough to point out that the notion of intention logically implies that of action, and therefore presupposes it, rather than vice versa. As an instance of the phenomenological theme of intentionality, one can say that an actor cannot 'intend'; she or he has to intend to do something. Moreover, of course, as everybody admits, there are many things that people do, that are brought about through their agency, which they do not do intentionally. The case of act-identifications I shall discuss in more detail subsequently, and I shall just categorically assert here that the characterization of action-types is no more logically derivable from intention than is the notion of action as such. However, we must be careful to separate the question of the general character of agency from that of the characterization of types of act; this is pointed out by Schutz, but is ignored in most Anglo-Saxon writings in the philosophy of action. Action is a continuous flow of 'lived-through experience'; its categorization into discrete sectors or 'pieces' depends upon a reflexive process of attention of the actor, or the regard of another. Although in the first part of this chapter I have not bothered to follow a strict differentiation, henceforth I shall refer to identified 'elements' or 'segments' of actions as *acts*, distinguishing these from 'action' or 'agency', which I shall use to refer generically to the lived-through process of everyday conduct. The idea that there are 'basic actions', which crops up in various forms in the philosophical literature, is a mistake which derives from not observing a distinction between action and acts. To talk of 'raising one's arm' is as much a categorization of an act as to talk of 'performing a blessing'; here we see another residue of the misleading opposition of action with 'movement'.[2]

I shall define action or agency as *the stream of actual or contemplated causal interventions of corporeal beings in the ongoing process of events-in-the-world*. The notion of agency connects directly with the concept of *Praxis*, and when speaking of regularized types of act I shall talk of human *practices*, as an ongoing series of 'practical activities'. It is analytical to the concept of agency: (1) that a person 'could have acted otherwise' and (2) that the world as constituted by a stream of events-in-process independent of the agent does not hold out a pre-determined future. The sense of 'could have done otherwise' is manifestly a difficult and controversial one, and aspects of it will be explored in various sections of this study. But it is evidently not on a par with the usual locutions, 'I had no choice', etc., and therefore with Durkheim's social 'constraint' or 'obligation'. A man who is obliged by the duties of his occupation to stay in his office on a sunny day is not in the same situation as one who is obliged to stay in his home by having broken both his legs. The same goes for forbearance, which involves the contemplation of a possible course of action – that which is refrained from. But there is one significant difference. While an ongoing stream of activity may, and very frequently does, involve reflexive anticipation of future courses of action, this is not necessary to the concept of action itself. Forbearance does, however, presuppose cognitive awareness of possible courses of action: it is not the same as simply 'not doing' things one could have done.

Intentions and projects

I shall use 'intention' and 'purpose' as equivalent terms, although everyday English usage recognizes distinctions between them. 'Purpose' in such usage, unlike 'intention', is not a wholly intentional term in the phenomenological sense: we speak of a person acting 'with purpose', or 'purposefully'. 'Purpose' seems to be related to 'resolve' or 'determination' in a way in which intention is not, implying that we tend to use the former word to refer to longer-term ambitions, while intention is more confined to day-to-day practices.[3] I shall, however, use the term 'project' to refer to such ambitions (for example, that of writing a book).

It is mistaken to presume, as some philosophers have done, that only those types of act can be called purposive of which actors themselves tend to ask for explanations in their everyday lives. Thus it has sometimes been claimed that since we do not usually ask someone to say what her intention was, for example, in putting salt on her dinner, such behaviour cannot be said to be intentional. Yet we might very well be inclined to make such an enquiry were she sprinkling her meal with talcum powder; and someone from another culture, where the custom is unfamiliar, might ask what the purpose of putting salt on the meal is. If we are not inclined to ask about it, this is certainly not because it makes no sense to pose such a question, but because we already know, or assume that we know, what her purpose is. The most mundane forms of day-to-day conduct can quite properly be called intentional. It is important to stress this, since otherwise it might be tempting to suppose that routine or habitual conduct cannot be purposive (as Weber tended to do). However, neither intentions nor projects should be equated with *consciously held-in-mind* orientations towards a goal – as if an actor must be aware of an aim he or she is seeking to attain. Most of the stream of action which constitutes everyday conduct is pre-reflective in this sense. Purpose does, however, presuppose 'knowledge'. I shall define as 'intentional' or 'purposive' *any act which the agent knows (believes) can be expected to manifest a particular quality or outcome, and in which this knowledge is made use of by the actor in order to produce this quality or outcome*. Note, however, that this presupposes a resolution of a problem to be approached later: that of the nature of act-identifications.

Some further points:

1   For action to be purposive, agents do not have to be capable of formulating the knowledge they apply as an abstract pro-position, nor does it have to be the case that such 'know-ledge' is valid.
2   Purpose is certainly not limited to human action. I do not think it useful or appropriate to hold that the concept can be stretched to cover any sort of homeostatic system. But much animal behaviour is purposive according to the conceptual-ization I have made.
3   Purpose cannot be adequately defined as some (for example, Toulmin) have suggested as dependent upon the application of 'learned procedures'.[4] While it is true that all purposive conduct, as I use the term, involves 'learned procedures' (knowledge that is applied to secure outcomes), there are also responses, such as conditioned reflexes, which are learned but not purposive.

The dislocation of purpose from agency can be shown in two ways: that agents may achieve their intentions, what they intended to do, but not through their agency; and that inten-tional acts characteristically bring about whole series of consequences, which are quite legitimately to be regarded as doings of the actors but were not actually intended by them. The first case is of little interest: it merely means that the in-tended outcome came about through some fortunate, unforeseen happening, not through the intervention of the agent as such. The second, however, is of great significance to social theory. The 'unintended consequences of intended acts' may take various forms. One is where the intended occurrence is not achieved, and instead the behaviour of the actor produces another outcome, or outcomes, which may come about either because the 'knowledge' applied as a 'means' is erroneous or irrelevant to the outcome that is sought, or because he or she is mistaken about the circumstances which are taken to call for the use of that 'means'.

Another is where the achievement of what was intended also brings about a range of other consequences. A person who switches on the light to illuminate the room perhaps also alerts a prowler.[5] Alerting the prowler is something the person *did*, although not something she intended to do. The examples which predominate in the philosophical literature of what has also been called the 'accordion effect' of action are of this simple kind. Notice that, first, the 'conclusion' of the chain appears an arbitrary one (if 'alerting the prowler' was something the actor 'did', was 'causing the prowler to flee' also something she 'did'?), and that, second, such examples do not help to illuminate those aspects of unintended consequences of most relevance to social theory, that is, those involved in what I shall later call the *reproduction of structure*.

The 'accordion effect' of action is not the same as what might be called the *hierarchy of purposes*, by which I mean the interlocking or interweaving of different purposes or projects. An act may be relevant to a number of intentions which the actor has in undertaking it; a project embodies a whole range of intentional modes of activity. The writing of a sentence on a sheet of paper is an act which relates also directly to the project of writing a book.

The identification of acts

It is generally accepted by most students of human conduct that such conduct has 'meanings', or is 'meaningful', in a way in which occurrences in the natural world are not. But a crude formulation of this sort will not suffice. For it is evident that the *natural world* is meaningful to us – and not just those aspects of nature which have been materially transformed and 'humanized'. We seek, and normally manage, to render the natural world 'intelligible' just as we do the social world – indeed, in Western culture the grounding of this intelligibility rests precisely upon the 'inanimate' character of nature, as determined by the operation of impersonal forces. It is often supposed that there is some kind of radical break between what is demanded in questions which ask for a clarification of the intelligibility of a happening and what is required in questions which ask for an explanatory, particularly a causal, account of that happening. And obviously there are differences. But they are not as clear-cut as one might be led to believe. To answer a question such as 'What was that sudden flash of light?' with the 'meaning' of the phenomenon – 'sheet lightning' – is at the same time to locate it within a scheme of likely aetiological accounts. The identification of the event as 'the occurrence of sheet lightning' takes for granted at least a rudimentary understanding of a relevant causal backdrop – one of a different sort to that presupposed by an answer like 'A message from the Great Spirit'. The frames of meaning whereby we make sense of events are never purely 'descriptive', but are closely interwoven with more thorough-going explanatory schemes, and the one cannot be cleanly prised loose from the other: the intelligibility of such descriptions depends upon these assumed links. The intelligibility of nature and natural events is accomplished by the construction and sustaining of frames of meaning from which the interpretative schemes whereby everyday experience is assimilated and 'handled' are derived. This is true of both laypeople and scientists; although in each case it would be a serious error to exaggerate the internal unity of such frames (cf. below, pp. 149ff). The understanding of descriptions generated within divergent frames of meaning – their *mediation* – in regard to the natural world is already a hermeneutic problem.

The difference between the social and natural world is that the latter does not constitute itself as 'meaningful': the meanings it has are produced by human beings in the course of their practical life, and as a consequence of their endeavours to understand or explain it for themselves. Social life – of which these endeavours are a part – on the other hand, is *produced* by its component actors precisely in terms of their active constitution and reconstitution of frames of meaning whereby they organize their experience.[6] The conceptual schemes of the social sciences therefore express a *double hermeneutic*, relating both to entering and grasping the frames of meaning involved in the production of social life by lay actors, and to reconstituting these within the new frames of meaning involved in technical conceptual schemes. I shall deal with some of the complicated issues raised by this at various later points in the book. But it is worthwhile pointing out at this juncture that the double hermeneutic of the social sciences places them in a quite different position to that of natural science in one basic respect. The concepts and theories produced in the natural sciences quite regularly filter into lay discourse and become appropriated as elements of everyday frames of reference. But this is of no relevance, of course, to the world of nature itself; whereas the appropriation of technical concepts and theories invented by social scientists can turn them into constituting elements of that very 'subject-matter' they were coined to characterize, and by that token *alter* the context of their application. This relation of reciprocity between common sense and technical theory is a peculiar, but eminently interesting, feature of social investigation.

The problem of the characterization of action-types immediately comes up against the difficulties posed by the double hermeneutic, and hence I shall first of all concentrate mainly upon the identification of acts within everyday conceptual frames, turning later (in the last chapter) to the relation between these and the technical concepts of social science.

Queries which prompt identifications of the meaning of events in nature, whether among lay observers or among scientists, are not of a unitary kind: that which is being asked for in the question 'What is happening?' is relative to, first, the interests that stimulate the enquiry, and, second, the level or type of knowledge already possessed by the enquirer (cf. Wittgenstein on ostensive definitions). The object or event exists or happens; but the characterization of it demanded in a query (it is not important here whether this is a question asked of another or of oneself) is dependent upon the above two considerations. The called-for answer to the question 'What have you got there?'

may be, in some circumstances, 'A book'; in another context it may be 'The new book by X'; or 'An object of a certain and definite mass'. All might be true characterizations, but there is no single one which is simply correct, the others being mistaken: it all depends upon the circumstances in which the query comes about.

The same thing holds in regard to queries oriented to identifications of human acts rather than of natural occurrences or objects. No end of trouble has been brought about by the tendency of philosophers to presume that the question 'What is X doing?' has a unitary answer; or that all answers to it must have a similar logical form. (In this respect it is definitely not the same as the question 'What is X intending to do?') For it soon becomes apparent that there are many possible responses to such a question: someone may be said to be 'bringing down a metal implement on wood', 'chopping logs', 'doing his job', 'having fun', etc. Since all of these are act-identifications, the philosopher then either looks for what they all have in common, or seeks to show that only some are 'correct' or 'valid' act-identifications and the others are not.[7] Yet all of these characterizations can be quite correct descriptions of what is going on – although, depending upon the context in which the query is formulated, only certain of them will be 'appropriate'. Picking up *which* is precisely one of the subtle skills which lay actors master as a routine characteristic of their participation in, and active production of, everyday interaction (and which they are able to manipulate to produce humour, irony, etc.).

It is evident that assumptions about purposiveness are as deeply intertwined with our characterizations of acts as beliefs about the causal features of impersonal forces are with our characterizations of natural events. Nevertheless, only a fairly restricted class of act-identifications logically presupposes that the type of doing must be intentional – such as 'suicide'. Most acts do not have this feature, that they cannot be done unintentionally. Of course, enquiries into an agent's conduct which seek not merely to characterize it intelligibly, but to penetrate to the individual's 'reasons' or 'motives' for what he or she does, certainly have to involve deciding what he or she was intending to do.

The rationalization of action

Ordinary English usage tends to elide distinctions between 'what-' and 'why-questions'. One might, in the appropriate context, ask either 'Why did that light suddenly flash across the sky?' or 'What was that sudden flash of light across the sky?' as equivalent sorts of enquiry; the answer 'It was sheet lightning' could be an acceptable one in either case. Similarly, act-identifications often serve as adequate responses to why-questions referring to human conduct. A person unfamiliar with British military procedure, seeing a soldier stiffly raising his hand to his forehead, might ask either 'What is he doing?' or 'Why is he doing that?'; to be informed that this is the mode of saluting in the British army might be enough to clarify the puzzle – that is to say, supposing the person were already familiar enough with what 'armies', 'soldiers', etc., are.

Distinctions between 'purposes', 'reasons' and 'motives' are also fuzzy in everyday discourse; these terms are quite often interchangeable. 'What was her purpose in doing that?' can be equivalent to 'What was her reason for doing that?' or 'What was her motive for doing that?' Most of those who have written on the philosophy of action are interested in arriving at clearer differentiations between these concepts than those recognized in everyday use; but the distinctions they have made by no means coincide. None the less, some such distinctions are necessary; those I propose to set out here develop the definition of intention or purpose which I have already established. Purposive conduct involves the application of 'knowledge' so as to produce a particular outcome or series of outcomes. To be sure, this is knowledge which is *applied*. But specification of which of an agent's doings are intentional necessarily involves establishing what the parameters of the knowledge which she or he applies are. Anscombe expresses this by saying that what is intentional 'under one description' is not intentional under another. A man may know, for example, that he is sawing a plank, but not that he is sawing Smith's plank.[8] Since it is analytical to the concept of an intended act that the agent 'knows' what he is doing, he cannot in this circumstance be said intentionally to have sawn

Smith's plank, even though he definitely did saw the plank on purpose and the plank was indeed Smith's. This is so even if the actor had temporarily forgotten the plank belonged to Smith at the time he was sawing it, and remembered afterwards. Human beings can provide us, directly or inadvertently, through what they say, with more or less clear-cut boundaries between which of their doings may be correctly called purposive, and which not; it is much more difficult to know where to draw such boundaries in the case of animal behaviour, where what 'knowledge' the animal applies has to be inferred.

The terms 'intention' and 'purpose' as such are rather misleading, or can easily become so, since they imply that the flux of the actor's life-activity can be clearly cut up into strings of intended outcomes. Only in rare circumstances does a person have a clear-cut 'end' in mind which organizes the energies unequivocally in one direction – for example, when the individual is set on winning a competitive game which, while he or she is playing it, completely absorbs the attention. In this sense the adjectives 'intentional' and 'purposive' are more accurate than their noun-forms. The purposive content of everyday action consists *in the continual successful 'monitoring' by the actor of her or his own activity*; it is indicative of a casual mastery of the course of day-to-day events that actors normally take for granted. To enquire into an actor's purposes for what he or she does is to enquire into in what ways, or from what aspects, the person is monitoring his or her involvement in the course of events in question. One's life-activity does not consist of a strung-out series of discrete purposes and projects, but of a continuing stream of purposive activity in interaction with others and with the world of nature; a 'purposive act', like act-identifications more generally, is only grasped reflexively by the actor, or isolated conceptually by another agent. It is in these terms that what I have referred to as the 'hierarchy of purposes' has to be understood; human agents are able to monitor their activities as various concurrent flows, most of which (as Schutz says) are 'held in stasis' at any point in time, but which the actor is 'aware' of, in the sense that he or she can recall them to mind as relevant to a particular event or situation that crops up.

What holds for 'intentions' and 'purposes' also applies to

'reasons'; that is, it is really appropriate to speak of the *rationalization of action* against the background of the agents' reflexive monitoring of their conduct. To ask for the reason for an act is to cut conceptually into the flow of action, which no more involves a strung-out series of discrete 'reasons' than it does such a series of 'intentions'. I have argued that purposive conduct may be usefully thought of as the application of 'knowledge' to secure certain outcomes, events or qualities. To enquire into the rationalization of such conduct, I shall say, *is to enquire into* (1) *the logical connection between various forms of purposive act, or projects, and* (2) *the 'technical grounding' of the knowledge that is applied as 'means' in purposive acts to secure particular outcomes.*

In spite of the overlap between the notions of 'purpose' and 'reason' in everyday usage, it is useful to separate out, in sociological analysis, various layers of enquiry which lay actors make into each other's activities. Where an actor's behaviour, 'what he is doing', is puzzling, another will first of all seek to make his behaviour intelligible by characterizing it meaningfully. However, she may be satisfied that she knows what the other is doing, and wish to ask what his purpose was in doing it, or if he did what he did intentionally at all (which may alter her initial characterization of the act, particularly where she is concerned with the attribution of moral responsibility: then 'killing' may become 'murder'). But she may wish to penetrate still more deeply than this, to the 'grounding' of what the actor did, which means asking about the *logical integration and the empirical content* of his monitoring of his activities.

'Reasons' may hence be defined as grounded principles of action, which agents 'keep in touch with' as a routine element of their reflexive monitoring of their behaviour. Let me offer an example from Schutz (cf. above, pp. 34–5): 'putting up an umbrella' is a characterization of an act; a person's intention in so doing might be expressed as 'to keep dry'; and the reason given for so doing as the awareness that a suitably shaped object held above the head will keep the rain off. A 'principle of action' thus constitutes an explanation of why a particular 'means' is the 'correct', 'proper' or 'appropriate' one to achieve a given outcome, as specified by a particular act-identification.

Expectation of the rationalization of 'technical effectiveness' in the reflexive monitoring of conduct is complemented by the expectation of logical consistency within what I have previously referred to as 'hierarchies of purpose': this is an integral feature of the rationality of action, because what is an 'end' (purpose) in relation to one act-identification may also be a 'means' within a broader project. In everyday life, agents' reasons, whether proffered directly or inferred by others, are clearly adjudged as 'adequate' in relation to the accepted parameters of common sense – of what is conventionally accepted in particular defined contexts of action.

Are reasons causes? This is one of the most hotly debated issues in the philosophy of action. Those who say reasons are not causes argue that the relation between reason and agency is a 'conceptual' one. There is no way, they claim, of describing what reasons are without referring to the conduct which they rationalize; since there are not two independent sets of events or states – that is, 'reasons' and 'actions' – there cannot be any question of the existence of any sort of causal relation connecting them. Authors, on the other hand, who have wished to make a case for the causal potency of reasons have looked for some way to establish their separation, as events, from the behaviour to which they relate. The matter obviously depends in some substantial part upon the notion of causality; I think it would be true to say that most of the contributions to the debate have been made, explicitly or otherwise, within a framework of Humean causality. A detailed discussion of the logic of causal analysis is impossible to undertake within the confines of this study, and here I shall dogmatically assert the need for an account of *agent causality*, according to which causality does not presuppose 'laws' of invariant connection (if anything, the reverse is the case), but rather (1) the *necessary connection* between cause and effect, and (2) the idea of causal efficacy. That action is caused by an agent's reflexive monitoring of his or her intentions in relation to both wants and appreciation of the demands of the 'outer' world, supplies a sufficient explication of freedom of conduct for the needs of this study; I do not therefore oppose freedom to causality, but rather 'agent causality' to 'event causality'. 'Determinism', in the social sciences, then refers to any theoretical scheme which reduces human action solely to 'event causality'.[9]

I have argued that talk of 'reasons' can be misleading, and that the rationalization of conduct is a basic feature of the monitoring intrinsic to the reflexive behaviour of human actors as purposive beings. Now in the conceptualization of these matters which I have developed, purposiveness is necessarily intentional, in the phenomenological sense – that is, 'logically' tied to descriptions of 'purposive acts' – but the rationalization of action is not, since this refers to the principled grounding of such acts. The rationalization of conduct expresses the causal anchoring of agency in tying purposes to the conditions of their realization within the ongoing *Praxis* of day-to-day life. Rather than simply saying reasons are, or may be, causes, it is more accurate to say that rationalization is the causal expression of the grounding of the purposiveness of the agent in *self-knowledge* and in *knowledge of the social and material worlds* which are the environment of the acting self.

I shall use 'motivation' to refer to the *wants* which prompt action. The connection of motivation to the affective elements of personality is a direct one, and is recognized in everyday usage; motives often have 'names' – fear, jealousy, vanity, etc. – and these are at the same time commonly regarded as the 'names' of emotions. Everything I have dealt with so far is 'accessible' to the *awareness* of the actor: not in the sense that she or he can formulate theoretically how she or he does what she or he does, but in the sense that, given that she or he is not dissimulating, her or his testimony as to the purpose and reasons for her or his conduct is the most important, if not necessarily conclusive, source of evidence about it. This does not hold in the case of motivation. As I shall use the term, it covers both instances where actors are aware of their wants, and also those where their behaviour is influenced by sources not accessible to their consciousness; since Freud, we have to reckon with the likelihood that the revealing of these sources may be actively resisted by the agent. The notion of *interest* stands in close relation to that of motive; 'interests' can be simply defined as any outcomes or events that facilitate the fufilment of agents' wants. There are no interests without wants: but since people are not necessarily aware of their motives for acting in a particular way, they are not necessarily aware of what, in any given situation, their interests are either. Neither, of course, do individuals inevitably act in accordance with their interests. Further, it would be wrong to suppose that intentions are always convergent with wants: a person may intend to do, and do, things which he or she does not want to do; and may want things that he or she does not intend to instigate any course of action to attain.[10]

Meaning and communicative intent

So far, I have been concerned only with problems of the 'meaning' of doings. When, in ordinary English usage, we refer to purposiveness we often talk about what a person 'means to do'; just as, in reference to utterances, we talk about what he or she 'means to say'. From this it would seem to be but a short step to the proposition, or the assumption, that to 'mean something' in doing is the same as to 'mean something' in saying. Here Austin's notions of illocutionary acts and illocutionary forces have done perhaps as much harm as good. Austin was struck by the fact that to say something is not always simply to state something. The utterance, 'With this ring I thee wed', is not a description of an action, but the very action (of marrying) itself. If, in such instances, to mean something in saying is *ipso facto* to mean something in doing, it would seem as though there is a single and sovereign form of meaning which does not necessitate making any differentiation between doing something and saying something. But this is not so. For virtually all utterances, with the exception of involuntary exclamations, cries of pain or ecstasy, have a communicative character. Some sorts of verbal communication, including ritual utterances such as 'With this ring I thee wed', are proclamatory in form, but this does not affect the point. In such cases the utterance is both a 'meaningful act' in itself, and is at the same time a mode of communicating a message or a meaning to others: the meaning in this case being perhaps something of the order 'the union of marriage is hereby sealed and made binding', as understood by the marital pair and others present on the scene.

The meaning of utterances as 'communicative acts' (if they have one) can thus always in principle be distinguished from the meaning of action, or the identification of action as particular acts. A communicative act is one in which an actor's purpose, or one of an actor's purposes, is linked to the achievement of passing on information to others. Such 'information', of course, does not have to be solely of a propositional sort, but can be comprised within an attempt to persuade or influence others to respond in a particular way. Now just as utterance may be both an act – something which is 'done' – and a 'communicative act', so something which is 'done' may also have communicative intent. The efforts that actors make to create specific sorts of impressions on others from the cues which they engineer their actions to 'give off' are well analysed in the writings of Erving Goffman, who is interested in comparing and contrasting such forms of communication with those conveyed in utterances. But again this does not detract from the point: chopping wood, and many other forms of action, are not communicative acts in this sense. There is, in sum, a difference between making sense of what someone is doing when she or he is doing something (including making ritual utterances in marriage ceremonies), and making sense of how others make sense of what she or he says or does in efforts at communication. I have noted that when actors or social scientists ask why-questions about actions, they may be asking either 'what' the action is, or for an explanation of why the actor should be inclined to conduct herself or himself in a particular way. We may ask such why-questions about utterances but when we want to know why a man said something in particular, rather than why he did something in particular, we are asking about his *communicative intent*. We may be asking what he meant, the first type of why-question; or we may be asking something such as 'What impelled him to say that to me in a situation when he knew it would embarrass me?'

Some, although only some, aspects of communicative intent in utterances have been explored by Strawson, Grice, Searle and others. The attempt to break away from older theories of meaning, represented by Wittgenstein's later studies, and by Austin's concentration on the instrumental uses of words, has undoubtedly had some welcome consequences. There is an obvious convergence between recent work in the philosophy of language and the ideas developed by Chomsky and his followers on transformational grammars. Both see language-use as a skilled and creative performance. But in some philosophical writings the reaction against the assumption that all utterances have some form of propositional content has led to an equally exaggerated emphasis in which 'meaning' comes to be regarded as exhausted by communicative intent.

In concluding this section, I want now to show that the work of the authors mentioned at the beginning of the previous paragraph leads us back to considerations given great prominence by Schutz and Garfinkel: the role of 'common-sense understandings', or what I shall later refer to as taken-for-granted *mutual knowledge*, in human social interaction. The most influential analysis of meaning as communicative intent ('non-natural meaning') is that given by Grice. In his original formulation, Grice put forward the view that the statement that an actor S 'meant so-and-so by X' is usually expressible as 'S intended the utterance X to produce an effect upon another or others by means of their recognizing this to be his intention'. But this will not do as it stands, he later pointed out, because it may include cases which would not be examples of (non-natural) meaning. A person may discover that whenever he or she makes a certain sort of exclamation another collapses in agony, and once having made the discovery, intentionally repeats the effect; if, however, when the first person makes the exclamation, the other collapses, having recognized the exclamation, and with it the intention, we should not want to say that the exclamation 'meant' something. Thus Grice reaches the conclusion that the effect which S intends to produce 'must be something which in some sense is within the control of the audience, or that in some sense of "reason" the recognition of the intention behind X is for the audience a reason and not merely a cause'.[11]

Various ambiguities and difficulties have been exposed in this account by critics. One of these is that it seems to lead to an infinite regress, in which what S_1 intends to produce as an effect upon S_2 depends upon S_1 intending S_2 to recognize his or her intention to get S_1 to recognize his or her intention to get S_2 to recognize his or her intention ... In his later discussion, Grice claims that the possibility of such a regress creates no particular problems, since in any actual situation the refusal, or incapacity, of an actor to proceed very far along the line of regressive knowledge of intentions will impose practical limits.[12] But this is not very satisfactory, since the problem of regress is a logical one; the regress can only be escaped, I think, by introducing an element that does not directly figure in Grice's own discussions. This element is precisely that of the 'common-sense under-standings' possessed by actors within shared cultural milieux – or, to adopt a different terminology, what one philosopher has called 'mutual knowledge'. (He says in fact that the phenomenon has no accepted name, and that hence he has to coin one.)[13] There are many things that an actor will assume or take for granted that any other competent agent will know when he addresses an utterance to her, and he will also take for granted that the other knows that he assumes this. This does not, I believe, introduce another infinite regress of 'knowing that the other knows that one knows that the other knows . . .'. The infinite regress of 'knowing that the other knows one knows . . .' threatens only in strategic circumstances, such as a poker game, in which the people involved are trying to out-manoeuvre or out-guess one another: and here it is a practical problem for the actors, rather than a logical one to puzzle the philosopher or social scientist. The 'common-sense understanding' or mutual knowledge relevant to the theory of communicative intent in-volves, first, 'what any competent actor can be expected to know (believe)' about the properties of competent actors, including both herself or himself and others, and second, that the particu-lar situation in which the actor is at a given time, and the other or others to whom an utterance is addressed, together comprise examples of a specific type of circumstance to which the attribu-tion of definite forms of competence is therefore appropriate.

The view has been strongly urged, by Grice and others, that communicative intent is the fundamental form of 'meaning', in the sense that giving a satisfactory account of it will allow us to understand the (conventional) meanings of utterance types. In other words, 'S-meaning' (what an actor means in making an utterance) is the key to explicating 'X-meaning' (what a specific mark or symbol means).[14] I want to deny that this is so. 'X-meaning' is both sociologically and logically prior to 'S-meaning'. Sociologically prior, because the framework of symbolic capacities necessary to the very existence of most human purposes, as these are acted upon by any individual person, presupposes the existence of a linguistic structure which mediates cultural forms. Logically prior, because any account which begins from 'S-meaning' cannot explain the origin of 'common-sense understandings' or mutual knowledge, but must assume them as givens. This can be made clear by looking at certain philosophical writings that mesh fairly closely with and have similar shortcomings to, Grice's theory of meaning.[15]

One such account, trimmed to its essentials, runs as follows. The meaning of a word in a linguistic community depends upon the norms or conventions which prevail in that community, to the effect that 'the word is conventionally accepted to mean p'. A convention can be understood as a resolution of a co-ordination problem, as the latter is defined in game-theory. In a co-ordination problem, two or more people have a shared end that they wish to bring about, to do which each has to select from a series of alternative, mutually exclusive means. The means selected have no significance in themselves, save that, combined with those chosen by the other or others, they serve to bring about what is mutually desired; the mutual responses of the actors are in equilibrium when there is an equivalence of outcomes, regardless of *what* means are used. Thus suppose two groups of individuals, one of whom is used to driving on the left, the other of whom is accustomed to driving on the right, come together to form a community in a new territory. The co-ordination problem is that of achieving the outcome that everyone drives on the same side of the road. There are two sets of equilibria that represent successful outcomes: where everyone drives on the right-hand side of the road, and where everyone drives on the left, and in terms of the initial problem as a problem of the co-ordination of actions, each is equally 'successful'. The significance of this is that it seems to indicate how communicative intent might be tied in with convention. For the actors involved in a co-ordination problem – at least, in so far as they conduct themselves 'rationally' – will all act in a way that they expect the others will expect that they will act.

But this view, while having a certain formal symmetry that is not unattractive, is misleading as an account of convention in general and as a theory of conventional aspects of meaning in particular. It is sociologically lacking, and I think logically untenable – in the latter respect in so far, at least, as it is focused on meaning conventions. In the first place, it seems evident that some sorts of norm or convention do not involve co-ordination problems at all. It is conventional in our culture, for example, for women to wear skirts and for men not to do so; but co-ordination problems are only associated with conventional styles of dress with regard to such matters in so far as, say, the fact that women now increasingly wear trousers rather than skirts creates a difficulty in telling the sexes apart, so that the achievement of mutually desired outcomes in sexual relationships may be compromised! More important, even in those conventions which might be said to involve co-ordination problems, the aims and expectations of those who are party to the conventions are characteristically defined *by* acceptance of the convention, rather than the convention being reached as an outcome of them. Co-ordination problems, as problems for *actors* (rather than for the social-scientific observer attempting to understand how the co-ordination of the actions of members is concretely realized), arise only in the circumstances I have already noted: when people are trying either to guess or to out-guess what others are going to do, having at their disposal the information that others are also trying to do the same with regard to their own likely actions. But in most circumstances in social life, actors do not (consciously) have to do this, in large part precisely *because* of the existence of conventions in terms of which 'appropriate' modes of response are taken for granted; this applies to norms as a whole, but with particular force to meaning conventions. When a person says something to another person, her or his aim is not that of co-ordinating her or his action to those of others, but of communicating with the other in some way, by the use *of* conventional symbols.

In this chapter, I have set out three main arguments. First, that neither the concept of action nor that of act-identification logically has anything to do with intentions; second, that the significance of 'reasons' in human conduct can best be understood as the 'theoretical aspect' of the reflexive monitoring of conduct which lay actors expect each other to sustain, so that if asked why he or she acted as he or she did, an actor is able to offer a principled explanation of the act; third, that the communication of meaning in interaction poses problems in some part separable from those concerning the identification of meaning in non-communicative acts.

In the following two chapters I shall be concerned to use and build upon the conclusions I have reached in this, which offer a preparatory basis for a reconstruction of the logic of social-scientific method. It is only preparatory because, as it stands, what I have said so far does not begin to deal with what, in my preceding critical discussion, I have isolated as some of the basic difficulties of 'interpretative sociology' – the failure to cope with problems of institutional organization, power and struggle as integral features of social life. In the next chapter, then, I shall attempt to integrate some of the contributions made by the various schools of thought previously discussed within the outlines of a theoretical scheme that is able satisfactorily to encompass these problems. A necessary preliminary to this, however, is a brief examination of why such a reconciliation is not already to be found in those established traditions of social theory which place issues of institutional analysis in the forefront: the 'orthodox academic sociology' of Durkheim and Parsons, and the counter-tradition originating in the writings of Marx. To this question I shall now turn.

3

The Production and Reproduction of Social Life

Order, power, conflict: Durkheim and Parsons

Durkheim's treatment of the 'externality' of social facts, and the 'constraint' which they exert over actors' conduct, was an attempt to provide a theory of the relation between action and the properties of social collectivities. When he first introduced the notions of externality and constraint, in *The Rules of Sociological Method*, Durkheim failed to separate out the general ontological sense in which the physical world has an existence independent of the knowing subject, and may causally influence his or her conduct, from the constraining properties of social organization. Later, however, he came to clarify the assumption, in fact already strongly developed even in his very first writings, that social phenomena are, in their very essence, *moral* phenomena. 'Utilitarian' sanctions, which influence human conduct in a 'mechanical' way, are distinguished from moral sanctions, whose content is specific to the moral universe to which they relate (the *conscience collective*); he came to hold that attachment to moral ideals is not merely constraining but is the very *source* of purposive conduct. In this latter aspect, a threefold connection is drawn: *social–moral–purposive*. This is the key to Durkheimian sociology, although it remains confused with a tendency to see some purposes as 'egocentric', based upon organic impulses, and as resistant to incorporation within the social universe of moral imperatives.[1]

Yet the view that purposes can be treated as 'introjected values' is by no means unique to Durkheim's writings; on the contrary, it appears in very many different places, and often in the works of those whose views are apparently quite distinct from, and indeed directly opposed to, those of Durkheim. The core axioms involved may be expressed as follows. The social world is differentiated from the world of nature essentially because of its moral ('normative') character. This is a very radical disjunction, because moral imperatives stand in no relation of symmetry to those of nature, and can hence in no way be derived from them; 'action', it is then declared, may be regarded as conduct which is oriented towards norms or conventions. This theorem can then lead in divergent directions, depending upon whether the analysis concentrates upon actors' purposes or motives, or whether the emphasis is placed, as by Durkheim, upon norms themselves as properties of collectivities. The post-Wittgensteinian philosophers have inevitably followed the first of these routes, approaching the study of purposive conduct via the assimilation of 'meaningful' with 'rule-governed' behaviour, leaving unexplained the origins of the rules to which they refer (as well as ignoring their character as *sanctioned*). The same course has been followed by numerous other recent writers who, although they are not themselves philosophers, have been influenced by the views of the professed followers of Wittgenstein. Thus in one such text we are told: 'Motives [by which the author means, in my terminology, "purposes"] are a way for an observer to assign relevance to behaviour in order that it may be recognized as another instance of *normatively ordered action*', or again: 'motive is a rule which depicts the social character of the act itself'.[2]

I have already indicated some of the flaws inherent in this sort of reasoning, and it is appropriate at this point to try to connect these up with the weaknesses involved in the one which is nominally its contrary: that is, that proposed by Durkheim – and followed in important respects more latterly by Parsons. Parsons's indebtedness to Durkheim in the formulation of his 'action frame of reference' is explicit and acknowledged. The main theme of *The Structure of Social Action* is that of an immanent convergence of thought between Alfred Marshall, Pareto,

Durkheim and Weber. Parsons discerns a parallel between Weber's treatment of action and Durkheim's concern with (internalized) moral obligation, which he then applies to provide a general resolution of 'Hobbes' problem of order'. The manner in which Parsons poses and seeks to resolve the Hobbesian problem' has two major sets of consequences whose implications I wish to discuss, involving: (1) the thesis that 'voluntarism' can be incorporated into social theory through the axiom that 'values' form both the motivational components of action and the core elements of the *consensus universel* which is the condition of social stability; (2) the assumption that conflict of interest in social life centres upon the relation between the 'individual' (abstract actor) and 'society' (global moral community) – a beginning-point which leads, as it did in Durkheim, straight to the view that dissent (crime, rebellion, revolution) is to be conceptualized as 'deviance', seen as lack of motivational commitment to consensual norms.

'Voluntarism'

Parsons's early work was directed towards reconciling the 'voluntarism' supposedly inherent in the methodological approach of Weber (and, from a different angle, foreshadowed in Pareto) with the idea of the functional exigency of moral consensus.[3] The notion of 'value', as it is represented in Parsons's writings, plays a key part in the 'action frame of reference' because it is the basic concept linking the need-dispositions of personality (introjected values) and (via normative role-expectations on the level of the social system) cultural consensus. 'A concrete action system', Parsons says, 'is an integrated structure of action elements in relation to a situation. *This means essentially integration of motivational and cultural or symbolic elements*, brought together in a certain kind of ordered system.'[4]

Once the significance of this idea is appreciated, it is not difficult to see why, as some have pointed out, the 'voluntarism' which appears prominent in Parsons's early work, *The Structure of Social Action*, seems to disappear from his mature position as described in *The Social System* and subsequent writings. As

Parsons represents it in the first work, voluntarism is counter-posed to 'positivism', the latter referring to nineteenth-century forms of social theory which sought to discard all reference to the acting subject as a moral actor, the former to those in which the acting subject is placed in the forefront. The use of the term 'voluntarism' suggests that Parsons wished to try to build into his own approach a conception of the actor as a creative, innovative agent. For Parsons the very same values that compose the *consensus universel*, as 'introjected' by actors, are the motiv-ating elements of personality. If these are the 'same' values, however, what leverage can there possibly be for the creative character of human action as nominally presupposed by the term 'voluntarism'? Parsons interprets the latter concept as referring simply to 'elements of a normative character';[5] *the 'freedom of the acting subject' then becomes reduced – and very clearly so in Parsons's mature theory – to the need-dispositions of personality.* In the 'action frame of reference', 'action' itself enters the picture only within the context of an emphasis that sociological accounts of conduct need to be complemented with psycho-logical accounts of 'the mechanisms of personality'. The system is a deterministic one.[6] Just as there is no room here for the creative capacity of the subject on the level of the actor, so there is a major source of difficulty in explaining the origins of transformations of institutionalized value-standards themselves – a problem which Parsons's system of theory (and that of Durkheim) shares with Winch's otherwise very different views about the philosophy of action, since both have to treat value-standards ('rules') as givens.

The individual in society

Parsons's resolution of the problem of order does of course recognize the existence of tensions or conflicts in social life. These derive from three possible sets of circumstances, each of which in some sense centres upon the notion of *anomie* – which is as integral to Parsons's thinking as it was to Durkheim's. One is the absence of 'binding value-standards' in some sphere of social life; the second is a lack of 'articulation', as Parsons puts it, between actors' need-dispositions and a given 'value-orientation pattern'; the third is where the 'conditional' elements of action, as perceived by an actor, are mistakenly specified. It has been said often enough that Parsons's theoretical scheme offers no place for interest-conflicts. In fact his very starting-point is the existence of interest-conflict, since the theorem of the integration of purposes and values is the main basis of his proposed resolution of 'Hobbes' problem of order', defined precisely in terms of the reconciliation of diverse and divergent interests. I have argued elsewhere that the 'Hobbesian problem' does not have the significance in the history of social thought which Parsons has claimed for it,[7] but it is important here to examine its analytical weaknesses. The point is not that Parsons's system (and that of Durkheim) allows no role to interest-conflict, but that it offers a specific, and flawed, theory of it, according to which clash of interests exists in so far as, and only in so far as, a social order fails approximately to match the purposes of the various members of a collectivity with the integration of value-standards into an internally symmetrical consensus. 'Conflict of interest', in this conception, never becomes anything more than a clash between the purposes of individual actors and the 'interests' of the collectivity. In such a perspective, power cannot become treated as a problematic component of divergent group interests embodied in social action, since the meshing of interests is treated first and foremost as a question of the relation between 'the individual' and 'society'.

Durkheim's views in this respect are more complex than those embodied in *The Social System* in at least one important way. Durkheim held that there are two primary modes in which the interests of actors may lead them to diverge from the moral imperatives of the *conscience collective*, although he did not manage fully to clarify the relation between these in his thought. One is based upon the role of organically given, egocentric impulses, which are conceived to be in constant tension with the moral demands of society, or the socialized segment of the dualistic personality of the actor. The other is the familiar scheme of the anomic lack of conjunction of actors' purposes with established moral norms. Durkheim's treatment of anomie offers some recognition of interest-conflict in so far as anomic 'deregulation' derives from a situation in which actors have definite aspirations which are not 'realizable' (an avenue later developed by Merton), rather than from a moral vacuum, an absence of moral norms which are binding upon actions.[8] But this possibility, which could have been linked to the analysis of what Durkheim referred to as the 'forced division of labour', and thereby to the analysis of class conflict, remained largely unexplored in Durkheim's writings, and disappears from view in Parsons's theoretical scheme altogether, since Parsons defines anomie as 'the polar antithesis of full institutionalization' or 'the complete breakdown of normative order'. Although Parsons's interpretation of the drift of Durkheim's thought offered in *The Structure of Social Action* is to my mind definitely a misleading one,[9] the above emphasis undoubtedly ties together the work of Durkheim and Parsons, thereby unifying one dominant tradition in sociology. The 'problem of order', from this angle, depends upon the centrality of a tension which is conceived to exist between 'egoism' and 'altruism': a problem of reconciling the sectional interests of individual actors with social morality, the *conscience collective* or 'common value system'. Given such an orientation to social theory, it is impossible satisfactorily to analyse the interests which intervene between the actions of individuals and the overall global community, the conflicts that are predicated upon these, and the power alignments with which they are interlaced.

The characteristic interpretation of 'order' as moral consensus appears very early in Parsons's work, and is attributed to Weber as well as Durkheim. Thus in commenting on his translation of Weber's discussion of legitimate order (*Ordnung*) Parsons remarks, 'it is clear that by "order" Weber here means a *normative* system. The pattern for the concept of "order" is not, as in the law of gravitation, the "order of nature".'[10] Whether Weber meant this or not, the 'problem of order' for Parsons is certainly one of normative regulation, a problem of *control*. The puzzle to which Parsons's formulations are offered as a solution is not equivalent in generality to Simmel's famous query: 'How is society possible?', which retains its significance if Parsons's presentation of the 'problem of order' is abandoned, as I hold it must be. If the term 'order' is to be used, I think, it should be in the sense which, in Parsons's comments on Weber mentioned above, it is implied is inappropriate to social science – as a loose synonym for 'pattern' or the antithesis of 'chaos'.

Order, power, conflict: Marx

In looking for an alternative to this type of theory, one tends to turn towards Marxism, with its apparently ubiquitous stress upon process, conflict and change. Two forms of dialectical relation in the movement of history may be distinguished in Marx's writings. One is a dialectic between humanity and nature; the other is a dialectic of classes. Both are linked to the transformation of history and culture. Human beings, unlike the lower animals, are not able to exist in a state of mere adaptation to the material world. The fact that the former do not possess an in-built apparatus of instinctual responses forces them into a creative interplay with their surroundings, such that they must seek to master their environment rather than simply adjust to it as a given; thus human beings change themselves through changing the world around them in a continual and reciprocal process. But this general 'philosophical anthropology' (which was not original to Marx and, in the form in which it was stated in the early writings in particular, does little more than to interject the 'Feuerbachian inversion' into Hegel's scheme) remains latent in Marx's subsequent works (with the partial exception of the *Grundrisse*, in which the reworking of these ideas is still fragmentary). Consequently there is little to be found in Marx in the way of a systematic analysis or elaboration of the basic notion of *Praxis*. We find statements like 'Consciousness is . . . from the very beginning a social product, and remains so as long as men exist at all' and, more specifically, 'Language is as old as consciousness, language *is* practical consciousness that exists also for other men . . . language, like consciousness, only arises from the need, the necessity, of intercourse with other men.'[11] Rather than exploring the implications of such propositions, Marx was principally interested in moving directly to the task of the historical interpretation of the development of particular types of society via the concepts of modes of production, division of labour, private property and classes, concentrating of course upon the critique of political economy and the optative transformation of capitalism by socialism.

Marx's discussions of material interest, conflict and power were worked out in this context, and reflect some of the ambiguities in the intellectual resources upon which they drew. It is clear enough that, within the capitalist order, the two major classes, capital and wage-labour, have divergent interests (both in the narrow sense of the appropriation of economic returns and in the more profound sense in which the interests of the working class promote the incipient socialization of labour, clashing with the entrenched defence of private property on the part of the dominant class); that these entail that class conflict, latent or manifest, is endemic in capitalist society; and that this condition of antagonism is more or less directly controlled or stabilized through the agency of the political power of the state. The transcendence of capitalism, however, marks the transcendence of classes, of their conflicts of interest, and of 'political power' itself. In this later regard, one can trace without difficulty the residual influence of Saint-Simon's doctrine, the idea that the administration of human beings by others will give way to the administration of humans over things. Marx's notion of the transcendence of the state is certainly vastly more sophisticated than that, as is evident in his remarks in his early critiques of Hegel, and his later comments on the Commune and the Gotha Programme. But classes, class interests, class conflict and political power are for Marx in a basic sense contingent upon the existence of a given type of society (class society), and since he rarely discusses 'interests', 'conflict' and 'power' outside of the context of classes, how far these concepts relate to socialist society is left obscure. *Class* interests and *class* conflicts may disappear in socialist society, but what happens to the interest divisions and conflicts which are not specifically linked to classes? There are statements in Marx's early writings which could be read as indicating that the arrival of communism signals the end of all forms of division of interest. We must surely presume that Marx did not hold such a view; but the absence of anything more than scattered hints about such matters makes it impossible to say much of a concrete sort about them. Now it may be pointed out that Marx refused to go into any detail about the society of the future on the grounds that such speculation degenerates into utopian socialism, since it is not possible to foresee the form of social organization that will characterize a society based on very different principles to the existing ones; and similarly it may perhaps be argued that concepts developed within one type of society – capitalism – would not be appropriate to the analysis of another – socialism. But these arguments do not detract from the main point: that the only cogent analyses of conflict and power in Marx link these specifically with class interests. From this aspect, Marx's writings do not provide an elaborated alternative to those main traditions of social thought whose 'philosophical anthropology' is centred upon the concepts of value, norm or convention.

What follows relies upon the fundamental idea of *the production and reproduction of social life*, which certainly appears consistent with the Marxian ontology of *Praxis*. In Marx's words: 'As individuals express their life, so they are. What they are, therefore, coincides with their production, both with *what* they produce and with *how* they produce.'[12] But 'production' has to be understood in a very broad sense, and in order to detail its implications we have to go well beyond what is immediately available in Marx's works.

The production or constitution of society is a skilled accomplishment of its members, but one that does not take place under conditions that are either wholly intended or wholly comprehended by them. The key to understanding social order – in the most general sense of that term which I have distinguished above – is not the 'internalization of values', but the shifting relations between the production and *reproduction* of social life by its constituent actors. *All reproduction is necessarily production*, however: and the seed of change is there in every act which contributes towards the reproduction of any 'ordered' form of social life. The process of reproduction begins with and depends upon the reproduction of the material circumstances of human existence: that is, the re-procreation of the species and the transformation of nature. Human beings, as Marx says, produce 'freely' in interchange with nature, in the paradoxical sense that they are *forced* actively to transform the material world in order to survive in it, since they lack an apparatus of instincts which would provide for a more mechanical adaptation to their material environment. But what above all distinguishes humans from the animals is that the former are able reflexively to 'programme' their environment, thereby monitoring their own place in it; this is made possible only by language, which is first and foremost the *medium of human practical activities*.

What are, analytically, the main conditions relevant to the reproduction of structures of interaction? These can be discussed as being of the following kinds: the constituting skills of social actors; the rationalization of these skills as forms of agency; the unexplicated features of settings of interaction that promote and permit the exercise of such capacities, which can be analysed in terms of *elements of motivation*, and what I shall call the *duality of structure*.

I shall develop the argument in the following sections of this chapter with reference to language, not because it is helpful to regard social life as some sort of language, information system or whatever, but because language, as a social form itself, exemplifies some aspects – and only some aspects – of social life as a whole. Language may be studied from at least three aspects of its production and reproduction, each of which is characteristic of the production and reproduction of society more generally. Language is 'mastered' and 'spoken' by actors; it is employed as a medium of communication between them; and it has structural properties which are in some sense constituted by the speech of a 'language community' or collectivity. From the aspect of its production as a series of speech acts by an individual speaker, language is (1) a skill, or very complex set of skills, that is possessed by each person who 'knows' the language; (2) used to 'make sense', literally, as a creative art of an active subject; (3) something which is *done*, accomplished, by the speaker, but not in full cognizance of how he or she does it. That is to say, the individual is likely to be able to offer only a fragmentary account of what skills are exercised, or of how they are exercised.

From its aspect as a *medium of communication in interaction*, language involves the use of 'interpretative schemes' to make sense not only of what others say, but of what they *mean*; the constitution of 'sense' as an *intersubjective* accomplishment of mutual understanding in an ongoing exchange; and the use of contextual cues, as properties of the setting, as an integral part of the constitution and comprehension of meaning. Considered as a *structure*, language is not 'possessed' by any particular speaker, but can be conceptualized only as characteristic of a community of speakers; it can be conceived of as an abstract set of rules which are not mechanically applied, but are employed in a generative mode by speakers who are members of the language community. Social life, I shall wish to say, then, may be treated as a set of *reproduced practices*. Following the threefold approach distinguished above, social practices may be studied, first, from the point of view of their constitution as a series of *acts*, 'brought off' by actors; second, as constituting forms of *interaction*, involving the communication of meaning; and third, as constituting *structures* which pertain to 'collectivities' or 'social communities'.

The production of communication as 'meaningful'

The production of interaction has three fundamental elements: its constitution as 'meaningful'; its constitution as a moral order; and its constitution as the operation of relations of power. I shall still for the moment defer consideration of the latter two, but only because they are so important as to warrant detailed treatment, and in the end these elements have to be reunited, since though they may be separated analytically, in social life itself they are subtly yet tightly interwoven.

The production of interaction as meaningful depends first of all upon mutuality of 'uptake' (Austin) in communicative intent, in which language is the primary but certainly not the only medium. In all interaction there is a constant interest in, and ability to disclose, modes of understanding of the conduct of the other apart from uptake of communicative intent – for example, in the understanding of motives. The subtleties of the everyday production of interaction can easily appear as merely peripheral nuisances if idealized models of dialogue as 'perfect mutual understandings' are treated as anything more than a possible world of philosophy only. Merleau-Ponty says: 'The will to speak is one and the same as the will to be understood.'[13] But whereas this presumably applies to itself as a statement of the philosopher, in everyday situations of interaction the will to speak is also sometimes the will to baffle, puzzle, deceive, be misunderstood.

It is essential to any adequate analysis of interaction as a product of the constituting skills of actors to recognize that its 'meaningfulness' is actively and continually negotiated, not merely the programmed communication of already established meanings: this, I take it, is the substance of Habermas's differentiation of 'linguistic' from 'communicative competence'. Interaction, as I have already emphasized, is temporally and spatially situated. But this is no more than an uninteresting truism if we do not see that it is typically used or *drawn upon* by actors in the production of interaction. Anticipations of the responses of others mediate the activity of each actor at any one moment in time, and what has gone before is subject to revision in the light of subsequent experience. In this way, as Gadamer emphasizes, practical social life displays ontologically the characteristics of the 'hermeneutic circle'. 'Context-dependence', in the various ways in which this term can be interpreted, is aptly regarded as integral to the production of meaning in interaction, not as just an embarrassment to formal analysis.

In relation to theories of definite descriptions, philosophers have frequently discussed the ambiguity of such sentences as 'A wants to marry someone of whom her parents disapprove.' But it is important to see that such discussions can become wholly misleading if set up as attempts to isolate an abstract logical structure from the communication of meaning in interaction. Here 'ambiguity' is ambiguity-in-context, and must definitely not be confused with the senses which a given word or sentence may have in circumstances other than those in which it is uttered by a particular speaker at a particular time. The sentence mentioned above is probably not ambiguous, for example, if uttered in the course of a conversation in which the individual figuring in the marriage plans of A has already been referred to; or alternatively if the course of such a conversation has made it clear to the participants that A was set on choosing a spouse who would prove objectionable to her parents, although having no one in particular in mind as yet. On the other hand, a statement which out of context might appear quite unambiguous, such as 'A is looking forward to getting married tomorrow', may in fact be ambiguous if, for example, uttered with a sufficient hint of sarcasm for a listener to be unsure whether or not the speaker 'means what he or she says'. Humour, irony and sarcasm all in some part depend upon such open possibilities of discourse, as recognized elements of the skills whereby interaction is constituted as meaningful.[14]

While such skills obviously involve 'knowledge' that is in principle capable of being expressed in propositional form, their saturation by temporal and spatial aspects of the context of communication is evidently not to be dealt with solely in these terms. Take an example discussed by Ziff. It is sometimes held by linguists that the meaning of a sentence such as 'The pen on the desk is made of gold', when used in an everyday context of communication, could be expressed in a formal language as a series of statements, known implicitly by the participants, describing 'relevant' contextual characteristics.[15] Thus the exact referent could be indicated by substituting for 'the pen on the desk', 'the only pen on the desk in the front room of number 10 Downing Street at 9.00 a.m. on the morning of 29 June 1992'. But as Ziff points out, such a sentence does not make explicit what was known to the participants in the encounter within which the utterance was made and understood, or used by them to produce the mutual understanding of the sentence. A hearer may be quite able to understand what was said, and the referent of the phrase, without being aware of any of the additional elements brought into the longer sentence at all. Moreover, it would be mistaken to suppose that, were everyday communication to be phrased in terms of sentences such as the longer one, there would be an increase in precision or a loss of ambiguity. The first sentence, uttered in a specific context, is neither imprecise nor ambiguous, whereas the use of the longer might bring about more vagueness and uncertainty, since it would extend the range of what has to be 'known' in common to accomplish the communication of meaning.

The use of reference to physical aspects of context is no doubt fundamental to the sustaining of an intersubjectively 'agreed upon' world within which most forms of day-to-day interaction occur. But 'awareness of an immediate sensory environment', as an element utilized in the production of interaction, cannot be radically severed from a backdrop of mutual knowledge drawn upon to create and sustain encounters, since the former is categorized and 'interpreted' in the light of the latter. I use the term 'mutual knowledge' to refer generically to taken-for-granted 'knowledge' which actors assume others possess, if they are 'competent' members of society, and which is drawn upon to sustain communication in interaction. This includes 'tacit knowledge', in Polanyi's sense; mutual knowledge is 'configurative' in character.[16] Even the most cursory verbal interchange presupposes, and draws upon, a diffuse stock of knowledge in the uptake of communicative intent. One person says to another: 'Do you want a game of tennis?', to which a second replies, 'I have work to do.' What is the connection between question and answer?[17] To grasp what has been said, 'by implication', it is necessary to know not merely what 'game' and 'work' mean as lexical items, but other much less easily formulated elements of knowledge of social practices which make the second utterance a (potentially) *appropriate* answer to the first. If the reply is not a particularly quizzical response, it is because it is mutually 'known' that work generally takes precedence over play when they conflict in the allocation of a person's time, or something of the sort. How far the questioner would 'let the response pass' as 'adequate' would of course depend upon a variety of circumstances particular to the situation in which the enquiry was made.

Mutual knowledge is applied in the form of *interpretative schemes* whereby contexts of communication are created and sustained in interaction. Such interpretative schemes ('typifications') can be regarded analytically as a series of generative rules for the uptake of the illocutionary force of utterances. Mutual knowledge is 'background knowledge' in the sense that it is taken for granted, and mostly remains unarticulated; on the other hand, it is not part of the 'background' in the sense that it is constantly actualized, displayed and modified by members of society in the course of their interaction. Taken-for-granted knowledge, in other words, is never fully taken for granted, and

the relevance of some particular element to an encounter may
have to be 'demonstrated', and sometimes fought for, by the
actor; it is not appropriated ready-made by actors, but is produced and reproduced anew by them as part of the continuity of
their lives.

Moral orders of interaction

The moral elements of interaction connect in an integral way
with its constitution both as meaningful and as a set of relations
of power. Each of these connections must be regarded as equally
basic. Norms figure in an important way in the writings of both
those who have taken a strongly naturalistic stance in social
theory (especially Durkheim) and those who have been their
most fervent critics. Although Durkheim came to elaborate his
original views in his later works, he nevertheless always tended
to stress the significance of norms as *constraining* or obligating:
to be approached through the notion of *sanctions*. Schutz, Winch
and others, on the other hand, have been more preoccupied with
the 'conferring' or 'enabling' qualities of norms. I wish to argue
that all norms are both *constraining* and *enabling*. I propose also
to distinguish between 'norms' and 'rules', which are casually
used as synonymous by most post-Wittgensteinian philosophers;
normative or moral rules I shall treat as a sub-category of the
more all-inclusive notion of 'rule', which I shall wish to connect
with that of 'structure'.

The constitution of interaction as a moral order may be understood as the actualization of *rights* and the enactment of
obligations. There is a logical symmetry between these which,
however, can be factually broken. That is to say, what is a right
of one participant in an encounter appears as an obligation of
another to respond in an 'appropriate' fashion, and vice versa;
but this tie can be severed if an obligation is not acknowledged
or honoured, and no sanction can effectively be brought to bear.
Thus, in the production of interaction, all normative elements
have to be treated as a series of *claims* whose realization is contingent upon the successful actualization of obligations through
the medium of the responses of other participants. Normative
sanctions are thus essentially different (as Durkheim recognized)

from those connected with the transgression of technical or utilitarian prescriptions, which involve what von Wright calls 'anankastic propositions'.[18] In prescriptions such as 'avoid drinking contaminated water', the sanction that is involved (the risk of being poisoned) follows 'mechanically' from the execution of the act: it depends upon causal relations that have the form of natural events.

In making this distinction, however, Durkheim neglected a vital sense in which norms may be approached in a 'utilitarian' fashion by participants in the production of interaction, and which must be conceptually related to the contingent character of the realization of normative claims. This is that a normative claim may be acknowledged as binding, not because an actor to whom it applies as an obligation accepts that obligation as a moral commitment, but because she or he anticipates, and wants to avoid, the sanctions which will be applied in the case of her or his non-compliance. In relation to the pursuance of her or his interests, therefore, an actor may approach moral claims in exactly the same way as she or he does technical prescriptions; in each case the individual may also 'calculate the risks' involved in a particular act in terms of the probability of escaping sanction. It is an elementary mistake to suppose that the enactment of a moral obligation necessarily implies a moral commitment to it.

Since the sanctions which follow the transgression of moral claims do not operate with the mechanical inevitability of events in nature, but involve the reactions of others, there is typically some 'free space' for the transgressor, if identified as such, to *negotiate* the character of the sanction which is to follow. This is *one* way in which the production of a normative order exists in close relation to the production of meaning: what the transgression *is* is potentially negotiable, and the manner in which it is characterized or identified affects the sanctions to which it may be subject. This is familiar, and formalized, in courts of law, but also pervades the whole arena of moral constitution as it operates in day-to-day life.

Sanctions are easily classified, on an abstract level, in terms of whether the resources which are mobilized to produce the sanction are 'internal': that is, involve elements of the actor's personality, or 'external': that is, draw upon features of the context of action. Each of these may be further categorized in terms of whether the resources which the sanctioning agent is able to mobilize are 'positive' or 'negative' with regard to the wants of the actor who is the target of sanction. Thus the actualization of 'internal' sanctions may draw upon a positive moral commitment of the actor, or negatively upon anxiety, fear or guilt; the actualization of 'external' sanctions may draw upon offers of reward or on the other hand may hold out the threat of force. Obviously, in actual situations of interaction several of these influences may operate simultaneously; and no 'external' sanction can be effective unless it brings into play an 'internal' one: a reward is only such if it impinges upon a person's wants.

The 'interpretation' of norms, and their capability to make an 'interpretation' *count* by participants in interaction is connected in subtle ways with their compliance to moral claims. Failure to see this, or at any rate to spell out its implications, is bound up with some characteristic defects of both Durkheimian–Parsonian functionalism and post-Wittgensteinian philosophy. The moral co-ordination of interaction is asymmetrically interdependent with its production as meaningful and with its expression of relations of power. This has two aspects, themselves closely associated with one another: (1) the possibility of clashes of different 'world-views' or, less macroscopically, definitions of what *is*; (2) the possibility of clashes between diverging understandings of 'common' norms.

Relations of power in interaction

The notion of 'action', I wish to claim, is *logically tied to that of power*. This is in a certain sense recognized by philosophers, who talk of 'can', 'is able to' or 'powers', in relation to the theory of action. But such discussions are rarely if ever related by their authors to the concept of power in sociology. The connection of 'action' to 'power' can be simply stated. Action intrinsically involves the application of 'means' to achieve outcomes, brought about through the direct intervention of an actor in a course of events, 'intended action' being a sub-class of the actor's doing or refraining from doing; power represents the capacity of the agent to mobilize resources to constitute those 'means'. In this most general sense, 'power' refers to the *transformative capacity* of human action, and I shall henceforth for the sake of clarity employ this second term, reserving the former one for a more restricted, relational use of 'power', to be further explicated below.

The transformative capacity of human action is placed in the forefront in Marx, and is the key element in the notion of *Praxis*. All systems of social theory have had to deal, in some way, with this – with the transformation of nature and the restlessly self-modifying character of human society. But in many schools of social thought the transformative capacity of action is conceived of as a dualism, an abstract contrast between the neutral world of nature on the one hand, and the 'value-laden' world of human society on the other. In such schools, particularly those associated with functionalism, with its emphasis upon social 'adaptation' to an 'environment', a grasp of historicity is easily relinquished. Only in the linked traditions of Hegelian philosophy and (certain versions of) Marxism has the transformative capacity of action, as the self-mediating process of labour, been made the centre-point of social analysis. Labour is, as Löwith says, 'a movement of mediation . . . a fashioning or "forming" and therefore positive destruction of the world which is present in nature'.[19] There seems little doubt that this broad emphasis remained basic to Marx's mature thought, although not significantly elaborated in it; in the *Grundrisse* we find affirmed, in language that closely echoes his early immersion in the 'brook of fire', that 'labour is the living, shaping fire; it represents the impermanence of things, their temporality, in other words their formation in the course of living time'.[20] However, Marx became increasingly preoccupied, not with labour as the transformative capacity of agency, but with its deformation as 'occupation' within the capitalist-industrial division of labour; and power as involved in social intercourse between people, as I have indicated in a preliminary way earlier, is analysed as a specific property of class relations rather than as a feature of social interaction in general.

'Power' in the sense of the transformative capacity of human agency is the capability of the actor to intervene in a series of events so as to alter their course; as such it is the 'can' which mediates between intentions or wants and the actual realization of the outcomes sought after. 'Power' in the narrower, relational sense is a property of interaction, and may be defined as the capability to secure outcomes where the realization of these outcomes depends upon the agency of *others*. It is in this sense that some have power 'over' others: this is power as *domination*. Several basic points have to be made here.

1   Power, in either the broad or restricted sense, refers to *capabilities*. Unlike the communication of meaning, power does not come into being only when being 'exercised', even if ultimately there is no other criterion whereby one can demonstrate what power actors possess. This is important, because we can talk of power being 'stored up' for future occasions of use.
2   The relation between power and conflict is a contingent one: as I have formulated it, the concept of power, in either sense, does not logically imply the existence of conflict. This stands against *some* uses, or misuses, of what is perhaps the most famous formulation of 'power' in the sociological literature, that of Max Weber, according to whom power is 'the capacity of an individual to realize his will, even against the opposition of others'.[21] The omission of the 'even' in some renderings of this definition is significant; then it becomes the case that power presupposes conflict, since power only exists when the resistance of others has to be overcome, their will subdued.[22]
3   It is the concept of 'interest', rather than that of power as such, which relates directly to conflict and solidarity. If power and conflict frequently go together, it is not because the one logically implies the other, but because power is linked to the pursuance of interests, and people's interests may fail to coincide. All I mean to say by this is that, while power is a feature of every form of human interaction, division of interest is not.
4   This does not imply that divisions of interest can be transcended in any empirical society; and it is certainly necessary to resist the linkage of 'interest' to hypothetical 'states of nature'.

The use of power in interaction can be understood in terms of resources or facilities which participants bring to and mobilize as elements of its production, thereby directing its course. These thus include the skills whereby the interaction is constituted as 'meaningful', but also – and these need only to be stated abstractly here – any other resources which a participant is capable of bringing to bear so as to influence or control the conduct of others who are parties to that interaction, including the possession of 'authority' and the threat or use of 'force'. It would be quite out of place to attempt to set out an elaborate typology of power resources in this study. My only concern at this point is to offer a generalized conceptual scheme which integrates the notion of power into the theoretical account developed in the present chapter. What it is necessary to do, however, is to relate this analysis of power back to the production of meaning in interaction.

This can best be accomplished by reverting briefly to Parsons's 'action frame of reference', or more specifically to criticism voiced about it by some of those influenced by ethnomethodology. Such criticism has taken roughly the following form. In Parsons's theory, it is argued, the actor is programmed to act as a result of values 'internalized' as need-dispositions of personality (in conjunction with non-normative 'conditions' of action). Actors are portrayed as unthinking dupes of their culture, and their interaction with others as the enactment of such need-dispositions rather than as, as it truly is, a series of skilled performances. I think this is right; but those who have expressed this sort of view have failed to pursue its consequences far enough. That is to say, following Garfinkel, they have been interested only in 'accountability', in the cognitive management of communication and communication settings. This is treated as the result of mutual 'labour' on the part of actors, but as if it were always the collaborative endeavour of *peers*, each contributing equally to the production of interaction, whose only interests are in sustaining an appearance of 'ontological security' whereby meaningfulness is constituted. In this one can trace the strong residual influence of Parsons's problem of order, but denuded of its volitional content, and reduced to a disembodied dialogue.

As against this, we must emphasize that the creation of frames of meaning occurs *as the mediation of practical activities*, and in terms of differentials of power which actors are able to bring to bear. The significance of this is crucial in social theory, which must find as one of its chief tasks the mutual accommodation of power and norms in social interaction. *The reflexive elaboration of frames of meaning is characteristically imbalanced in relation to the possession of power*, whether this be a result of the superior linguistic or dialectical skills of one person in conversation with another; the possession of relevant types of 'technical knowledge'; the mobilization of authority or 'force', etc. 'What passes for social reality' stands in immediate relation to the distribution of power – not only on the most mundane levels of everyday interaction, but also on the level of global cultures and ideologies, whose influence indeed may be felt in every corner of everyday social life itself.[23]

Rationalization and reflexivity

I have already pointed out that in most traditional schools of social thought reflexivity is treated as merely a nuisance, the consequences of which either can be ignored or are to be minimized as far as possible. This is true both in respect of methodology, where 'introspection' is swingeingly condemned as contrary to science, and in respect of the conceptual representation of human conduct itself. But nothing is more central to, and distinctive of, human life than the reflexive monitoring of behaviour, which is expected by all 'competent' members of society of others. In the writings of those social thinkers who do not acknowledge this as central, there is an odd paradox, often pointed to by their critics: for recognition of their very 'competence' as authors involves just what is obliterated in the accounts they offer of the behaviour of others.

No actor is able to monitor the flow of action exhaustively, and when asked to explain why she did what she did at a particular time and in a particular place, may choose to reply 'for no reason' without in any way compromising others' acceptance or her as 'competent'. But this only applies to those aspects of day-to-day interaction which are accepted as trivial, not to anything deemed important in an agent's conduct, for which the actor is always expected to be able to supply reasons if they are asked for (I shall not consider here how far this observation might apply outside the realm of Western culture). Since the giving of reasons involves the actor in providing a verbal account of what may only implicitly guide her or his behaviour, there is a thin line between 'rationalization' as I have used the term, and 'rationalization' meaning the giving of false reasons after the event. The giving of reasons is embroiled in the assessment of moral responsibility for acts, and hence easily lends itself to dissimulation or deceit. To recognize this, however, is not the same as holding that all reasons are merely 'principled explanations' offered by actors about what they do, in the light of accepted canons of responsibility, regardless of whether these were in some sense incorporated into their doings.

There are two senses in which reasons may be held by actors to be 'valid', and the interlocking of these is of no small consequence in social life. One is how far an agent's stated reasons in fact express the person's monitoring of what he or she did; the other is how far his or her explanation conforms to what is generally *acknowledged*, in that individual's social milieu, as 'reasonable' conduct. The latter, in turn, depends upon more or less diffusely integrated patterns of belief which actors refer to in order to derive principled explanations of each other's conduct. What Schutz calls the 'stock of knowledge' which actors possess, and apply in the production of interaction, actually covers two analytically separable elements. There is what I have called generically 'mutual knowledge', which refers to the interpretative schemes whereby actors constitute and understand social life as meaningful; this can be distinguished from what I shall call 'common sense', which can be seen as comprising a more-or-less articulated body of theoretical knowledge, drawn upon to explain why things are as they are, or happen as they do, in the natural and social worlds. Common-sense beliefs typically underpin the mutual knowledge which is brought to any encounter by participants; the latter depends in a basic way upon a framework of 'ontological security' supplied by common sense.

Common sense is by no means solely practical in character – 'cookery-book knowledge'. It is normally in some substantial degree derived from, and responsive to, the activities of 'experts', who make the most direct contribution to the explicit rationalization of culture. 'Experts' include all those who have the authority of privileged entrée to realms of specialized knowledge – priests, magicians, scientists, philosophers. Common sense is certainly in part the accumulated wisdom of laypeople; but common-sense beliefs just as certainly reflect and embody the perspectives developed by experts. As Evans-Pritchard remarks, the individual in European culture regards rain as the result of 'natural causes' which could be set out by a meteorologist, but is unlikely to be able to offer anything more than a rudimentary explanation of this sort; a Zande characterizes the origins of rain within a different cosmology.[24]

The rationalization of action via common sense is a phenomenon of far-reaching importance to sociology, since social scientists themselves lay claim to be experts who are purveyors of authoritative 'knowledge'. This therefore raises the crucial question: in what sense are the 'stocks of knowledge', which actors employ to constitute or make happen that very society that is the object of analysis, corrigible in the light of sociological research and theory? Without prejudicing later discussion of this on an abstract level, we must first of all consider two aspects from which actors' conduct may be opaque to themselves: first, that of motivation and, second, that of the structural properties of social totalities.

The motivation of action

It would be wrong to suppose that the kinds of explanation that actors look for, and accept, regarding the behaviour of others are limited to the rationalization of conduct, that is, to where the actor is presumed to understand adequately what she or he is doing and why she or he is doing it. In ordinary English usage, as I have previously mentioned, 'reasons' are not clearly distinguished from motives: one might ask 'What was his reason for doing Y?' as an equivalent to 'What was his motive for doing Y?' Nevertheless, it is recognized that to enquire into someone's motives for acting as he does is potentially to seek elements in his conduct of which the actor might not fully be aware himself or herself. This is why, I think, the term 'unconscious motives' does no particular violence to ordinary English usage, whereas 'unconscious reasons' seems rather less easy to accept. My use of 'motivation', therefore, as referring to wants of which an actor may or may not be conscious, or may only become aware after he or she has carried out the act to which a particular motive refers, in fact conforms quite closely to lay usage.

Human motivation may be aptly conceived of as *hierarchically* ordered, both in a developmental sense and in terms of the distribution of wants at any given time in the life of the person. An infant is not a being capable of reflexivity: the capacity for the monitoring of one's own activities is predicated firmly and fundamentally upon the mastery of language, although this does not preclude the possible validity of Mead's thesis that reflexivity is on its most primitive level grounded in the reciprocity of social relations in the interaction of the infant with other members of the family group. Now although the very young infant may know a few words, which serve as signs in interaction with others, a child does not attain a broad command of linguistic skills, or a mastery of the intricacies of the deictic terminology of 'I', 'me' and 'you', until somewhere between two and three years of age. Only as this occurs is she or he able, or expected, to attain the rudiments of the ability to monitor her or his own conduct in a manner akin to that of an adult. But while a child is not born a reflexive being, it is born one with wants, a set of organic needs for the provision of which it is dependent upon others, and which mediate its expanding involvement in a definite social world. The earliest period of 'socialization', therefore, can be presumed to involve the development of the capacity for 'tension management' on the part of the infant, whereby it is able actively to accommodate its wants to the demands or expectations of others.

Given that the modes of management of organic wants represent the first, and in an important sense the most all-embracing, accommodation which the child makes to the world, it seems legitimate to suppose that a 'basic security system' – that is, a primitive level of management of tensions rooted in organic needs – remains central to later personality development; and given that these processes occur first of all before the child acquires the linguistic skills necessary to monitor its learning consciously, it also seems reasonable to hold that they lie 'below' the threshold of those aspects of conduct that, learned later and in conjunction with the reflexive monitoring of such learning, are easily verbalized – thus 'made conscious' – by the older child or adult. Even the earliest learning of the infant is understood in a misleading sense, however, if conceived of as mere 'adaptation' to a pre-given external world; the infant is from the first days of its life a being that actively shapes the settings of its interaction with others and, having wants that may in some part clash with those of others, can become involved in interest-conflict with them.

That human wants are hierarchically ordered, involving a core 'basic security system' largely inaccessible to the consciousness of the actor, is of course not an uncontroversial assertion, and is one which shares a great deal with the general emphasis of psychoanalytic theory; but it does not imply a commitment to the more detailed elements of Freud's theoretical or therapeutic scheme.

The maintenance of a framework of 'ontological security' is, like all other aspects of social life, an ongoing accomplishment of lay actors. Within the production of modes of interaction in which the mutual knowledge required to sustain that interaction is 'unproblematic', and hence can be largely 'taken for granted', ontological security is routinely grounded. 'Critical situations' exist where such routine grounding is radically dislocated, and where consequently the accustomed constituting skills of actors no longer mesh in with the motivational components of their action. The 'security of being' which is largely taken without question in most day-to-day forms of social life is thus of two connected kinds: the sustaining of a *cognitively* ordered world of self and other, and the maintenance of an 'effective' order of want management. Tensions and ambivalences in motivation can derive from either of these sources, and as such can be analysed as conflicts within and between 'layers' in the stratification of wants.

The production and reproduction of structure

The true locus of Weber's distinction between 'action' and 'social action' is in the differentiation of action from acts carried out with some kind of communicative intent, the second of these being the necessary condition of interaction. Mutuality of orientation in this respect may be regarded as a defining characteristic of interaction, anything else – for example, a man's adoration of a film star who is unconscious of his existence – being a limiting case of action. Two points need to be made here that will have to be more fully developed later.

1 Communicative intent, that is, the production of 'meaning' in this sense, is only one element of interaction; it is equally important, as I have indicated, that every interaction is also a *moral* and a *power relation*.
2 Collectivities 'consist of' interactions between members but structures do not; any system of interaction, however, from a casual encounter up to a complex social organization, may be analysed structurally.

An approach to the analysis of structure in sociology can be made by comparing what I will now simply call 'speech' (action and interaction) with 'language' (structure), the latter being an abstract 'property' of a community of speakers. This is not an *analogy*: I am definitely not claiming that 'society is like a language'. (1) Speech is 'situated', that is, spatially and temporally located, whereas language is, as Ricoeur puts it, 'virtual and outside of time'.[25] (2) Speech presupposes a subject, whereas language is specifically subject-less – even if it does not 'exist' except in so far as it is 'known' to, and produced by, its speakers. (3) Speech always potentially acknowledges the presence of another. Its relevance as facilitating communicative intent is fundamental, but it is also the intended medium, as Austin makes clear, of a whole host of other 'illocutionary effects'; (natural) language as a structure, on the other hand, is neither an intended product of any one subject, nor oriented towards another. In sum, generalizing this, practices are the situated doings of a subject, can be examined with regard to intended outcomes, and may involve an orientation towards securing a response or range of responses from another or others; structure, on the other hand, has no specific socio-temporal location, is characterized by the 'absence of a subject', and cannot be framed in terms of a subject–object dialectic.

In most versions of what has come to be called 'structuralism', and particularly in the writings of Lévi-Strauss, 'structure' is not regarded as a descriptive concept: a structure is discerned in myth through applying rules of transformation which penetrate the level of appearances. The parentage of this standpoint in Saussurian linguistics is well known, and however brilliant its achievements in the formal dissection of mythologies, it bears the limitations of its origins in its inability to confront issues of the genesis and temporality of meaning. Lévi-Strauss was apparently prepared, at one time at least, to accept Ricoeur's representation of his views as 'Kantianism without a transcendental subject', disavowing this as a criticism. He has subsequently recoiled from this position, but still seems unconcerned about 'bracketing out the acting subject'.[26]

In 'functionalism', from Spencer and Durkheim through Radcliffe-Brown and Malinowski to Parsons and his followers, on the other hand, 'structure' is used in descriptive, and largely unexamined ways; it is 'function' which is called upon to play the explanatory role. The introduction of the notion of function as an explanatory element in Durkheim's sociology excluded temporality from major areas of social analysis, in so far as history (and causation) was severed from function. I have argued elsewhere that Durkheim was far more of an historical thinker than is generally recognized today.[27] One reason this is not often acknowledged is that, once he had methodologically separated history – happenings in time – and function, he was unable to recombine them. One looks in vain for any systematic account of social change in Durkheim that is connected theoretically to his functional analyses of moral integration; change appears only as an abstract scheme of types of society in an evolutionary hieararchy.

It is surely true that these emphases reappear also in Parsons's writings, and it is as well to consider the inadequacies of functionalism at source in Durkheim, who, in a way characteristic of much nineteenth-century social thought, drew upon 'organic analogies'. I shall make no attempt to trace through the career of the concept of function at the hands of Merton, etc., since I propose to abandon the notion completely. The separation of function (relations between 'parts' of a 'whole') from seriality (happenings in time) that Durkheim sought to draw cannot be sustained; a functional relation cannot even be stated without implied reference to temporality. In the analogy from physiology upon which Durkheim's account is based, we may say that the heart stands in a functional relation to the rest of the body, contributing to the overall perpetuation of the life of the organism; but what such a statement conceals is reference to a series of events in time: the heart's pumping of the blood through the arteries conveys oxygen to other parts of the body, etc. *A structure can be described 'out of time', but its 'functioning' cannot.* In physiology, statements couched in terms of functional relations can always in principle be transcribed into statements of causal connections without residue: the causal properties of blood flow, etc. The chief interest of 'functional analysis' is not really anything to do with 'wholes' and 'parts' at all, but is in the postulation of *homeostasis*. This, however, is readily reconceptualized as a problem of the *reproduction* of structure: as in the constant replacement of the cells of the skin in a physiognomy which – through this very process – maintains its structural identity.

It has to be made clear that use of 'structure' in social theory is not necessarily implicated in the failings of either structuralism or functionalism, in spite of its terminological association with them: neither school of thought is able to grapple adequately with the constitution of social life as the production of active subjects. This I shall seek to do through introducing the notion of *structuration* as the true explanatory locus of structural analysis. To study structuration is to attempt to determine the conditions which govern the continuity and dissolution of structures or types of structure. Put in another way: *to enquire into the process of reproduction is to specify the connections between 'structuration' and 'structure'.* The characteristic error of the philosophy of action is to treat the problem of 'production' only, thus not developing any concept of structural analysis at all; the limitation of both structuralism and functionalism, on the other hand, is to regard 'reproduction' as a mechanical outcome, rather than as an active constituting process, accomplished by, and consisting in, the doings of active subjects.

A structure is not a 'group', 'collectivity' or 'organization': these *have* structural properties. Groups, collectivities, etc., can and should be studied as systems of interaction, and there seems little doubt that systems-theoretical concepts can be applied fruitfully within the social sciences. Systems theory has only superficially penetrated the vocabulary of social science, and it is essential to make clear the difference between it and traditional notions of homeostatic systems as, for instance, characteristically employed in functionalism. Reciprocal effects tending to the establishment of equilibrium, such as may be involved in mechanical or organic systems, are not examples of autopoesis proper. The differences are actually threefold.

1 Equilibrium tendencies working through reciprocal effects operate 'blindly', not through control centres by means of which input and output are mutually assessed and co-ordinated.
2 The notion of homeostasis presupposes a static interdependence of parts, and is able to conceive of change in the system only in terms of a strain to equilibrium versus a strain toward disintegration (function versus dysfunction in a 'net balance of functional consequences' in Merton's phrase), not in terms of the internal self-transformation of the system.
3 In homeostatic systems of 'functional interdependence' each functional relation is usually regarded as equivalent to every other: in social systems, however, it is vital to recognize degrees of interdependence, since relations of interdependence are always and everywhere also relations of power.

I have already indicated that structure is 'subject-less'. Interaction is constituted by and in the conduct of subjects; *structuration*, as the reproduction of practices, refers abstractly to the dynamic process whereby structures come into being. By the *duality of structure* I mean that social structure is both constituted *by* human agency and yet is at the same time the very *medium* of this constitution. In sorting out the threads of how this happens, we can again profit initially by considering the case of language. Language exists as a 'structure', syntactical and semantic, only in so far as there are some kinds of traceable consistency in what people say, in the speech acts which they perform. From this aspect to refer to rules of syntax, for example, is to refer to the reproduction of 'like elements'; on the other hand, such rules also *generate* the totality of speech-acts which is the spoken language. It is this dual aspect of structure, as both inferred from observations of human doings and yet also operating as a medium whereby those doings are made possible, that has to be grasped through the notions of structuration and reproduction.

The duality of structure in social interaction can be represented as follows:

INTERACTION	Communication	Power	Morality
(MODALITY)	Interpretative scheme	Facility	Norm
STRUCTURE	Signification	Domination	Legitimation

What I call 'modalities' refer to the mediation of interaction and structure in processes of social reproduction; the concepts on the first line refer to properties of interaction, while those on the third line are characterizations of structure. The communication of meaning in interaction involves the use of interpretative schemes by means of which sense is *made* by participants of what each says and does. The application of such cognitive schemes, within a framework of mutual knowledge, depends upon and draws from a 'cognitive order' which is shared by a community; but while drawing upon such a cognitive order the application of interpretative schemes at the same time *reconstitutes* that order. The use of power in interaction involves the application of facilities whereby participants are able to generate outcomes through affecting the conduct of others; the facilities both are drawn from an order of domination and at the same time, as they are applied, reproduce that order of domination. Finally, the moral constitution of interaction involves the application of norms which draw from a legitimate order, and yet by that very application reconstitute it. Just as communication, power and morality are integral elements of interaction, so signification, domination and legitimation are only analytically separable properties of structure.

Structures of signification can be analysed as systems of *semantic rules* (or conventions); those of domination as systems of *resources*; those of legitimation as systems of *moral rules*. In any concrete situation of interaction, members of society draw upon these as modalities of production and reproduction, although as an integrated set rather than three discrete components. When related to a totality of collectivities, as an integrated *system* of semantic and moral rules, we can speak of the existence of a common culture. The modes in which actors draw upon semantic and moral rules in the constitution of interaction can be generally treated in the manner of Wittgenstein's analysis of rule-following. That is to say, to know a rule is not to be able to provide an abstract formulation of it, but to know how to apply it to novel circumstances, which includes knowing about the *contexts* of its application. However, we have to be careful to acknowledge the limits of the game-analogies which are used to express the fusion of language-games and forms of life in the *Philosophical Investigations*, and which have been employed so often by philosophers of action subsequently. The rules of games are usually of a distinctive sort. The boundaries within which they apply – the 'play-sphere' – are typically clearly delimited and unquestioned. Moreover, they constitute a unified whole in that they are more or less rationally co-ordinated with one another. There are a few other social practices, namely rituals and ceremonials, which also tend to have a 'closed' character (Huizinga, Caillois and others have pointed out that the sacred displays close similarities to play), and do not generate much change from within themselves just because they are set apart from the ordinary interests of day-to-day life. But most rule-systems must not be assumed to be like this. They are less unified; subject to chronic ambiguities of 'interpretation', so that their application or use is *contested*, a matter of *struggle*; and constantly in process, subject to continual transformation in the course of the production and reproduction of social life. Hence the importance of examining the organization of resources which, on the level of interaction, actors are capable of drawing upon as sanctions; and which, on the level of structural integration, support divergent ideologies.

Processes of structuration tie the *structural integration or transformation* of collectivities or organizations as systems to the *social integration or transformation* of interaction on the level of the life-world. But it is important to recognize that forms of the integration of interaction do not necessarily directly parallel the systems which they serve to reproduce. Hence there is a need to differentiate *conflict* from *contradiction*. The notion of conflict is closely tied to that of 'interest' (although not necessarily so, since actors may mistake where their interests lie), which logically presupposes that of the 'wants' which actors bring to interaction. Conflict, in the sense of active struggle pursued in the context of clashes of interest, is a property of interaction. Contradiction, on the other hand, may be understood as a structural quality of the collectivity, and as standing in contingent relation to conflict. Contradiction can be conceptualized as the opposition between structural 'principles': for example, between the fixed allocation of labour characteristic of feudalism and the free mobility of labour stimulated by emergent capitalist markets at a certain period in European history. Now in order to avoid treating contradiction as equivalent to 'functional incompatibility', it is essential to recognize that such 'principles' *always* entail an implicitly or explicitly acknowledged distribution of interests on the level of social integration – for example, that a certain category of actors (entrepreneurs) have interests in promoting the mobility of labour, while others (feudal landowners) have opposing interests. But the occurrence of conflict on the level of social integration does not necessarily produce system contradiction; and the existence of contradiction is not inevitably expressed as overt struggle.

To speak of 'structure' and 'structuration', in sociological analysis, is not equivalent to speaking in the *reified mode*, which has to be treated as a phenomenon of the life-world of lay actors. In the reified mode, collectivities figure in the language of their members as entities that are produced, not by people themselves , but as alien objects in nature and are thus dislocated from their character *as* human products. The terminology of structure and structuration acknowledges a distinction between objectification (*Vergegenständlichung*) and reification. Failure to observe such a distinction is the characteristic mark of idealism in social theory. The dissolution of reification is evidently tied to the possibility of the (cognitive) realization by actors that structures are their own products; and to the (practical) recovery of their control over them. These two implications of the transcendence of reified modes of thought are easily confused, however. Just such a confusion lends credence to rationalistic social criticism: the thesis that awareness of the conditions of human social life leads *ipso facto* to the achievement of control.

Summary

A few summary comments on the themes of this chapter might be useful. I began by suggesting several respects in which Durkheim's sociology and Parsons's 'action frame of reference', although directed towards many of the issues which are covered in this study, are unsatisfactory. Although Parsons employs the term, his scheme in fact fails to develop a theory of action, as I have defined the notion; it allows for division of interest in social life only in terms of an opposition of the 'individual' and 'society', seen as a moral community; and the origins of social conflict are correspondingly traced to imperfections in the moral commitments which tie the motivation of individual actors to the 'central values' upon which social stability depends. Marx's writings appear to offer a very different framework of analysis, in which power, division of interest and struggle appear as the leading features; but because of his concentration upon the critique of the political economy of capitalism, to which he gave over his life's work, Marx never managed to return to the more general problems of ontology that preoccupied him in the early part of his intellectual career. Consequently Marx's works offer only a broad preliminary orientation, in respect of the notions of *Praxis* and the transformative capacity of human labour, to the specific concerns with which I wish to deal.

The production of society, I have argued, is always and everywhere a skilled accomplishment of its members. While this is recognized by each of the schools of interpretative sociology that I have discussed in the first part of this study, they have not managed successfully to reconcile such an emphasis with the equally essential thesis, dominant in most deterministic schools of social thought, that if human beings make society, they do not do so merely under conditions of their own choosing. In other words, it is fundamental to complement the idea of the production of social life with that of social reproduction. Speech and language provide us with a series of useful clues as to how to conceptualize processes of social production and reproduction – not because society is like a language, but on the contrary because language as a practical activity is so central to social life that in *some* basic respects it can be treated as exemplifying social processes in general. Speech (action) presupposes a subject (actor), and speech acts are situated contextually – as is dialogue between speakers (interaction). Speech and dialogue are each complex accomplishments of their producers: knowing how to produce them, on the other hand, is very definitely not the same as being able to specify either the conditions which make possible their production or the unintended consequences which they might be instrumental in bringing about. Considered in terms of its structural properties – and this is crucial – (natural) language is a condition of the generation of speech acts and the achievement of dialogue, but also the unintended consequence of the production of speech and the accomplishment of dialogue. This *duality of structure* is the most integral feature of processes of social reproduction, which in turn can always be analysed in principle as a dynamic process of *structuration*. Analytically, three elements of the production of forms of interaction can be distinguished: all interaction involves (attempted) communication, the operation of power, and moral relations. The modalities whereby these are 'brought off' in interaction by participating actors can also be treated as the means whereby structures are reconstituted.

By the term 'structure' I do not refer, as is conventional in functionalism, to the descriptive analysis of the relations of interaction which 'compose' organizations or collectivities, but to systems of generative rules and resources. Structures exist 'out of time and space', and have to be treated for purposes of analysis as specifically 'impersonal'; but while there is no reason why the sorts of theoretical apparatus which have been developed to analyse the behaviour of open systems should not be applied to the structure of collectivities, it is essential to recognize that structures only exist as the reproduced conduct of situated actors with definite intentions and interests. Thus, for example, the identification of 'contradiction' on the level of system integration is only possible because it implicitly presupposes recognition of opposition of interest on the level of situated forms of inter-action: it is precisely this which separates the notion of contradiction here from the notion of 'functional incompatibility' as formulated in functionalist theory. Two points should perhaps be stressed to avoid misunderstanding.

1   To say that structure exists 'out of time and space' is only to claim that it cannot be treated as the situated doings of concrete subjects, which it both serves to constitute and is constituted by; not, of course, that it has no internal history.

2   The concept of reproduction no more has a special connection to the study of social 'stability' than it has to that of social 'change'. On the contrary, it helps to cut across the division between 'statics' and 'dynamics' so characteristic of functionalism from Comte until modern times. Every act which contributes to the reproduction of structure is also an act of production, a novel enterprise, and as such may initiate change by altering that structure at the same time as it reproduces it – as the meanings of words change in and through their use.

The concept of motivation is important to social theory in three ways. First, motivational elements may operate as un-acknowledged causal conditions of action – that is, as unconscious impulses unavailable to the reflexive monitoring of the rationalization of conduct. In principle, the relation between such elements, and an actor's ongoing rationalization of his or her behaviour, must be regarded as plastic, as offering the possibility of the revelatory development of self-understanding. Second, motives generate definite *interests*. While the notion of 'interest' has to be understood very broadly, as referring to any course of action that facilitates the achievement of wants, the more significant sense in social analysis is that of 'social interest', where a response of *others* serves as a means to the pursuance of particular interests. Third, the theory of motivation is immediately relevant to that of the reproduction of structure. As I tried to show at the beginning of this chapter, however, the thesis of the correspondence of motives and the 'internalization' of consensual values, as set out by Parsons, is an inadequate version of such a theory. This is so for two reasons.

1   It is derived from the 'Hobbesian problem of order', which, predicating a state of nature in which every person's hand is set against every other, is only able to cope with division of interest in society in so far as this is represented as a division between the interests of individual actors and those of the social community as a whole.
2   Motivational commitment to a given 'order' is made equivalent to moral commitment to that 'order', thus pushing to the margins a concern with accommodation to it as a system of domination which both expresses, and is reproduced by, asymmetries of power in social interaction.

4

The Form of Explanatory Accounts

In nineteenth-century social philosophy and social theory positivism was in the ascendant, if positivism is taken to mean two things. First, a conviction that all 'knowledge', or all that is to count as 'knowledge', is capable of being expressed in terms which refer in an immediate way to some reality, or aspects of reality that can be apprehended through the senses. Second, a faith that the methods and logical form of science, as epitomized in classical physics, can be applied to the study of social phenomena. In the writings of Comte and Marx alike, the science of social life was to complete the freeing of the human spirit from religious dogmas and customary, unexamined beliefs. I have already talked of the erosion in the twentieth century of faith in scientific knowledge as the exemplar of all knowledge, and of the ranking of human cultures according to how far they have progressed towards the attainment of scientific rationalism. With the tempering, or loss, of the conviction that scientific knowledge is the highest form of knowledge, and the only sort worth striving to attain, has come a reappraisal of traditional and habitual beliefs and modes of action, formerly largely dismissed as a compound of unthinking custom and blind prejudice.

In philosophy, one result was a massive split between two streams of thought in the 1920s and 1930s. On the one hand, logical positivism arose as a more radical defence of the privileged status of scientific knowledge than had ever been developed before. On the other hand, in phenomenology and linguistic philosophy, the authority of common sense was resurrected and placed in the forefront as both a topic of study and a resource for study. The phenomenological philosophers have sought to effect a critique of natural science by arguing that its claims to knowledge are secondary to, and dependent upon, ontological premises of the natural attitude. Linguistic philosophy, on the other hand, has not generated any such critique, but rather has tended to cut itself off from the philosophy of science by insisting that there exists a logical disparity between the social world and the world of nature, confining its attentions to the former. Both phenomenology and linguistic philosophy culminate in a critique of social science, however, from the point of view of the 'natural attitude'.

The technical defence of common sense by phenomenological and 'ordinary language' philosophers, in so far as this is directed towards explicating problems of the social sciences, converges with what might be regarded as a very common common-sense attitude towards them. According to such a view, the findings of social science, and especially of sociology, are bound to be unremarkable, since they cannot do more than redescribe what we must already know as participants in social life – thus, as Louch, a philosopher I have already quoted, puts it, sociologists' accounts of social conduct must 'seem unnecessary and pretentious'. This idea is normally dismissed fairly casually by social scientists themselves, who offer two reasons for its rebuttal. One is that even if it were true that sociology merely 'describes', or 'redescribes', what actors already know about their actions, no specific person can possess detailed knowledge of anything more than the particular sector of society in which he or she participates, so that there still remains the task of making into an explicit and comprehensive body of knowledge that which is only known in a partial way by lay actors themselves. However, most would go on to add, it is in any case not true that their endeavours can be no more than descriptive in character; their aim is to correct and improve upon notions used by actors themselves in interpreting their own actions and the action of others. I think that this is indeed so. But, in the face of the critiques developed in the interpretative sociologies, discussed in chapter 1, the claim demands detailed elucidation. Such elucidation confronts an array of epistemological problems of considerable complexity.

Positivistic dilemmas

Comte coined both the terms 'positive philosophy' and 'sociology', thus establishing a conjunction which, if it did not serve to accomplish the practical social reforms he envisaged, none the less consolidated an intellectual tradition that had a great deal of influence in sociology. The thesis that there can be a 'natural science of society' which, whatever the differences between human conduct and occurrences in nature, would involve explanatory schemes of the same logical form as those established in the natural sciences, has been elaborated in various guises. Durkheim's *Rules of Sociological Method* remains perhaps the boldest expression of such a view, and it is worth briefly characterizing the framework of inductive method that it advocates. According to Durkheim, the object of sociology is to construct theories about human conduct inductively on the basis of prior observations about that conduct: these observations, which are made about externally 'visible' characteristics of behaviour, are necessarily 'pre-theoretical', since it is out of them that theories are born.

Such observations, it is held, have no particular connection with the ideas actors have about their own actions and those of others; it is incumbent upon the observer to make every possible effort to keep them separate from common-sense notions held by actors themselves, because these frequently have no basis in fact. In Durkheim's presentation of this standpoint, the social scientist is instructed to formulate his or her concepts at the outset of research and to break away from those current in everyday life. The concepts of everyday activity, Durkheim says, 'merely express the confused impression of the mob'; 'if we follow common use,' he continues, 'we risk distinguishing what should be combined, or combining what should be distinguished, thus mistaking the real affinities of things, and accordingly misapprehending their nature'. The investigations which the social scientist makes have to deal with 'comparable facts', whose 'natural affinities' cannot be distinguished by the 'superficial examination that gives rise to ordinary terminology'. The assumption that there are discriminable 'natural affinities' of objects (physical or social), which pre-exist and determine what the observer does in describing and classifying those objects, appears throughout Durkheim's writings. What this actually leads to is classification by fiat – which has, not surprisingly, disturbed many of his readers. Thus, for example, having dismissed commonsense notions of suicide as irrelevant to his study, Durkheim proceeded to establish a new definition of the phenomenon, as he put it, 'to determine the order of facts to be studied under the name of suicides'.

The ideas worked out in *Suicide* are thus supposedly based upon the initial formulation of the nature of suicide, defined as 'all cases of death resulting directly or indirectly from a positive or negative act of the victim himself, which he knows will produce this result'.[1] But, it has been argued by critics, such a definition is impossible to apply. One reason given for this is that Durkheim was unable to observe the distinctions entailed in his own formulation, because virtually all of his analyses involve the use of suicide statistics, and it seems rather unlikely that the officials who constructed those statistics understood by 'suicide' what Durkheim proposed the term should be used to mean. The more radical claim has also been made by some of the critics mentioned in chapter 1 that a concept of 'suicide' such as might be employed in social analysis must be constructed out of detailed descriptions of relevant common-sense concepts used by actors themselves. Now I shall want to affirm subsequently that the problem of 'adequacy', involving the relation between everyday language and social scientific metalanguages, is an issue of basic importance. However, no useful end is served by supposing that, in place of the 'external affinities' between social phenomena that Durkheim sought, we can merely substitute ideations. While this view is quite different in substance from the Durkheimian sort of programme, in logical form it is quite similar to it. For it is an assumption of both that social science has to be founded upon descriptions of 'reality' that are 'pretheoretical' in character. In the case of those influenced by phenomenology, this is a 'reality' composed of ideas, rather than 'external' characteristics of conduct. Once we have ascertained what this reality 'is' – for example, 'suicide' as defined as a phenomenon by members of society – we are supposedly in a position to build up generalizations on that basis, although there is some considerable difference of opinion about what kinds of generalization these will be.

In so far as they concern general matters of epistemology, the issues involved here can be illuminated by reference to the long-standing debate over the status of 'observational statements' in the philosophy of natural science. What Feigl called the 'ortho-dox' view of natural science, as formulated by those influenced by logical positivism, ran roughly as follows. Scientific theories are hypothetico-deductive systems. The creation of theories involves several levels of conceptual differentiation – at the highest level, abstract postulates which cannot be given a precise definition in terms of their empirical content, but only in terms of their logical relations with other postulates. The concepts contained in theoretical generalizations are distinct from the terms of the observation language, which refer to the sensory 'soil' of observation as given in experience. Hence there have to be correspondence rules which specify the relations that pertain between the language of observation and the language of theory.[2] According to such a view, as well as to earlier-established variants of empiricism, the 'data' of experience force upon us definite modes of description and classification of the world of 'outer reality'. This implies two claims: that it is feasible and necessary to search for some sort of ultimate foundations of scientific knowledge which are 'certain'; and that these foundations have to be located in some area of experience which can be described or categorized in a language which is theoretically neutral.

The quest for foundations of empirical knowledge has occupied Western philosophers since Descartes, and has been pursued in modern times by empiricists and phenomenologists alike. Both come up with answers that presuppose an essentially passive relation between subject and object: in the first case, the bedrock is found in sense-experience, in the second, it is found in ideations that are regarded as distinct from experience and instead inform it. The first, however, having located its 'starting-point' in sensory experience, finds difficulty in explaining the nature of theoretical categories, which do not stand in any discernible relation of isomorphy with sense-data, and hence it becomes necessary to introduce correspondence rules which connect the content of one to the content of the other. This has never been satisfactory, for the nature of correspondence rules has proved elusive. The other view, having located the foundations of knowledge in the ideal categories that are immediately available to the ego, finds the reverse difficulty – that of reconstituting the world of sensory experience itself.

Each of the claims mentioned in the above paragraph can be disputed. Most traditional schools of philosophy have proceeded on the assumption that our choice of a 'starting-point' is decisively important to scientific knowledge, since the foundations determine the character of all that is built upon them. But there can be no foundations of knowledge that are unshakeably secure, or which are not theory-impregnated. The idea of a 'protocol language' – as Quine once put it, a 'fancifully fancyless medium of unvarnished news' – depends upon what Popper sardonically labels the 'bucket theory of knowledge': the human mind is treated as if it were a sort of container, empty at birth, into which material pours through our senses, and in which it accumulates.[3] All immediate experience, it is held, is thus received as sense-data. There are many objections that can be made to this, as Popper indicates in his devastating critique. Statements which refer to 'sensory observation' cannot be expressed in a theoretically neutral observation language; the differentiation between the latter and theoretical language is a relative one, within a framework of a pre-existing conceptual system.

Later developments: Popper and Kuhn

In the English-speaking world (where the partially convergent developments in France, via the works of Bachelard, Canguilhem and others did not become well known),[4] Popper's writings stand in a peculiar tension in relation to logical positivism on the one hand – both in its original formulation within the Vienna circle, and in its subsequent emendation and elaboration in the hands of Carnap, Hempel and others in the United States – and to the 'newer philosophy of science' (Kuhn, Lakatos and Feyerabend) on the other.[5] Although this seems not to have been fully acknowledged at the time by those close to the Vienna circle, it seems clear that *The Logic of Scientific Discovery*, in its original version, broke radically with the tenets of logical positivism. In place of the attempted reduction of meaning to testability, Popper substituted the twin themes of the establishment of criteria of demarcation – separating science from other forms of belief or enquiry – and the significance of falsification within a framework of deductive logic. From the joining of these two themes the whole thrust of Popper's philosophy of science follows, with its emphasis upon boldness and ingenuity in scientific innovation, and upon the significance of critical rationalism among the professional body of scientists.

The critical reception of Popper's own work is by now well advanced, as a result of the contributions of Kuhn and others and the debates which they have stimulated, and also as a consequence of the controversy over Popper's writings in Germany.[6] Popper's philosophy of science broke substantially not only with logical positivism, but also with traditional conceptions of science which tended to treat scientific method in terms of the individual scientist confronting a subject-matter, substituting for this a recognition of science as a collective enterprise, an institutionalization of critical reason. But, precisely because of this latter emphasis, Popper's work also prepared the way for Kuhn and for subsequent developments in the philosophy of science that in some substantial part moved away from Popper's own views.

The reception of Kuhn's writings in the social sciences has been a curious one. The term 'paradigm' has been picked up by many authors, but applied either loosely as synonymous with 'theory', or in the more confined sense that Merton once gave to the term.[7] Some such authors have then concluded, surveying sociology, that the latter has no single, universally accepted paradigm. But that is hardly illuminating, since one of the things which led Kuhn to formulate the notion of paradigm in the first place, and to apply it to the development of the natural sciences, was his perception of deep-rooted disagreements about basic premises that seemed to him to characterize social science, but not natural science – except in certain major phases of transformation.[8] (It is of some interest, and perhaps not entirely irrelevant, to remark that an endeavour to distinguish scientific knowledge from *certain* traditions in social science – namely Marxism and psychoanalysis – also provided the driving impetus to Popper's philosophy of science.)[9] The significance of the concept of 'paradigm', in Kuhn's sense, is that it refers to a series of very basic, taken-for-granted understandings that form a frame for the conduct of 'normal science'. As such, however, in the context of its use in *The Structure of Scientific Revolutions*, the concept has brought to the surface a series of major epistemological problems that in large part are shared by the natural and social sciences, and stand logically prior to features that may divide them.

Before reverting to matters specific to the social sciences, therefore, I shall concentrate upon such general problems of epistemology, including in particular those centring upon 'incommensurability' and relativism.

There are at least two respects in which Kuhn's work, together with the subsequent writings of those influenced by him, introduce basic difficulties for Popper's standpoint.

1 Kuhn's formulation of 'normal science' suggests that the development of science, outside of certain 'revolutionary phases' of change, depends upon a suspension of critical reason – the taking for granted of a set of epistemological propositions – rather than upon the immanent 'permanent revolution' of critical reason which is at the heart of Popper's philosophy of science. The issues separating Kuhn and Popper on this point concern less whether or not 'normal science' exists than whether its existence positively facilitates, or inhibits, scientific 'progress'. For Kuhn, the suspension of critical reason in respect of the underlying premises of paradigms is a necessary condition for the successes of natural science; for Popper, 'normal science' is a subversion of the norms of critical exchange to which alone science owes its distinctive character as contrasted to dogma or myth.

2 The writings of Kuhn and others demonstrate that scientists often either ignore or 'explain away' results of experiments or observations that are later generally acknowledged as being inconsistent with – or as falsifying – accepted theories. Such results may be treated as compatible with a theory when initially produced, but appear to later workers as quite irreconcilable with it; or recognized as inconsistent with the theory at its current stage of development, but 'laid aside' as capable of explanation in terms of a revised version of the theory at a subsequent date.

The difficulties which are thus presented for the notion of falsification in the Popperian philosophy of science connect directly to issues raised by Winch (and, in an earlier generation, by Lévy-Bruhl) concerning the similarities and differences between Western science and religious or magical practices in non-industrialized societies. For, as Evans-Pritchard has shown so brilliantly, Zande sorcery possesses a cosmology which is readily able to deal with what – to an outsider – may appear to be 'non-confirming' instances. If one person seeks, through magical means, to injure or kill another, and that other person remains in the best of health, explanation as to how this could be so is readily to hand. Something unknown 'went wrong' on this particular occasion when the oracle was consulted; the ritual incantation was not performed perfectly correctly; or the second person enjoyed access to stronger magic than the first, and was able to render the other's efforts ineffective. In what sense then, if any, is Western science able to lay any claim to an understanding of the world that is more grounded in 'truth' than that of the Azande, who perhaps simply operate with a different overall cosmology (read: 'paradigm') to that of science?

Science and non-science

In answering this question, it is vital to separate a number of logically distinct, if related, problems: (1) how science is to be differentiated from non-science – in particular, religion and magic, on the level of social organization; (2) the 'grounding' of science epistemologically; (3) the significance of falsification as a principle of scientific procedure; (4) the mediation of paradigms within the context of the development of science.

Differentiation from non-science

It is apparent from discussions of African cosmologies that the distinctiveness of the social organization of Western science is not easily characterized. Such cosmologies are able to provide internally consistent, comprehensive 'explanatory accounts' of happenings in the world; they may make some sort of place for self-criticism and for the revision of the claims to knowledge that they generate. If it be granted that most Western science approximates to Kuhn's 'normal science', involving assumptions, largely taken for granted, within which 'puzzle-solving' is the order of the day; and that science, like religion and magic, is in substantial part oriented towards practical ends, helping to generate definite forms of technology – then the activities of scientists and sorcerers seem to parallel each other rather closely. Now it is important to emphasize these parallels; appreciation of them helps to undermine the sort of intellectual arrogance in the face of other types of claim to knowledge that logical positivism showed in its early years. But this is quite a different matter from glossing over the differences which separate religion and magic (in so far as it is legitimate to generalize so grossly, ignoring the diversity of traditional cosmologies) from science. I shall comment on these only briefly.

Among the differences which separate Western science from *most* types of religious and magical practice are these. First, science operates within a world-view that treats happenings in 'nature' as the outcome of impersonal forces. Now the very word 'force' seems originally to have religious origins, and it is not uncommon to find concepts of impersonal force (*mana*) in religious or magical systems: but most also involve personalized gods, spirits or demons. Second, science institutionalizes the public display, within professional communities, of modes whereby theories are formulated and observations are made.

The ideals whereby scientific enterprise is legitimated, involving free debate and critical testing, may not coincide with actual practice. But both ideals and practice are at some distance from even the most liberal forms of religion or magic. In the latter, doctrinal disputes certainly occur frequently. But religion and magic rarely seek rational self-transformation on the basis of the critical reception of documented observations. This central legitimating feature of science often becomes dogma; but it is one absent from most religious doctrines. Finally, religion and magic often, although not at all universally, involve forms of activity that are alien to Western science: including worship in regularized ceremonial, propitiation and sacrifice.

Epistemological grounding of science

Such sociological comparisons are of no immediate relevance, however, to the epistemological grounding of science – the so-called 'basis-problem'. The difficulties with Popper's position here are well known. How are we to find a rational basis for critical rationalism? The commonly offered solution to this question – that a commitment to critical reason can be grounded self-referentially, if that commitment be regarded as itself open to rational debate, and therefore the possibility of rejection – is hardly adequate. We have to recognize, in the face of such attempts, that any endeavour to ground the rationalism of science within the logic of science as such finds itself in a logical circle. But this is only a vicious circle if its closing is treated as an end-point of enquiry, rather than as a beginning. There is *no way* of justifying a commitment to scientific rationality rather than, say, to Zande sorcery, apart from premises and values which science itself presupposes, and indeed has drawn from historically in its evolution within Western culture. Whether such a commitment involves a Kierkegaardian 'leap into faith', or can alternatively be handled within a framework of critical theory, raises issues of very great complexity which it is beyond the compass of this study to discuss.

The significance of falsification

Popper's critique of inductive logic in the philosophy of science, in its original version, ran in outline as follows. Inductive logic is closely linked to empiricism and to the sort of model of scientific method described by Bacon. The patient observation of happenings in the world discloses regularities which, having been verified by repeated empirical tests, are then stated as universal laws. Yet this notion of the verification of laws is subject to a notorious embarrassment: no matter how many tests are carried out, the law cannot be said to be certainly verified, since there always remains the possibility that the $n + 1^{th}$ observation, following a finite series, will be inconsistent with it. The conviction that scientific knowledge is the most secure type of knowledge that we can attain thus stands at odds with the logical impossibility of ever conclusively verifying scientific laws. By abandoning the idea of induction, Popper attempts to break free also from the perspective according to which science is founded upon the dull discipline of careful fact-gathering, and replace it with the thesis that science advances above all through the bold and daring conjecture of 'implausible' hypotheses that are readily open to potential falsification.

The critical response to Popper has shown conclusively that 'falsificationism' cannot be sustained in its original form. According to Popper's famous example, the universal law 'all swans are white' can never be verified, since this would demand access to the total population of swans, past, present and future; but it can be falsified by the discovery of a single black swan. However, matters are not so simple. The discovery of a black swan might not falsify the law: a swan that had been painted black, or dipped in soot, would not qualify as a falsifying instance;[10] nor, if this were possible, would the discovery of a black animal born of the union of a swan and a black eagle, since this would probably not count as a 'swan', even if it were like a swan in most important respects. What these instances show is that 'all swans are white' presupposes theories of the origins of colour-typing and biological form in birds. What 'counts' as a falsifying observation thus depends in some way upon the theoretical system or paradigm within which the description of what is observed is couched; and such theoretical systems are able to provide the sorts of accommodation to apparently falsifying instances that I have mentioned previously.

This being so, one can ask whether, deprived of the simplicity which gives the argument much of its attractiveness and logical power, falsificationism in the philosophy of science should be abandoned in favour of a reversion to a more traditional framework of verification and inductive logic. The issue is a difficult one, because the idea of falsification in Popper's writings is so closely bound up with his critical rationalism (in social philosophy as well as in the philosophy of science). I shall offer only the following comments.

1   It is of fundamental importance to sustain the break with empiricism, in respect of the denial of a theory-free language of observation, regardless of the difficulties that this may create for the formula of falsification.
2   The thesis that science is – or should strain toward being – bold, innovating, yet always retaining an essential radical scepticism toward those of its findings that at any time appear most firmly established, is equally basic. I shall revert at a later point to the bearing of Kuhn's arguments upon this.
3   'Simple falsificationism' thus has to be replaced by a more 'sophisticated falsificationism' – which Lakatos in fact claims, not entirely convincingly, to discover in Popper's own writings.[11] Lakatos' formulation of 'degenerative' versus 'progressive problem-shifts' is probably the most adequate treatment of these issues worked out in the contemporary literature in the philosophy of science. The development of a novel research programme in science is 'progressive' if it is more comprehensive, predicts and explains 'new facts', and resolves inconsistencies or 'blank spots' in the one which it replaces. Lakatos' revised scheme of falsificationism, however, shares the broad limitations of the Popperian philosophy of science to which it is connected. For he offers no indication of how the criteria of what is to count as a 'progressive problem-shift' are themselves to be grounded epistemologically.

Paradigms

Kuhn's use of 'paradigm', and some of the difficulties to which it leads, although nominally confined to the history and philosophy of science, clearly share certain elements in common with notions developed in otherwise rather divergent philosophical traditions: 'language-games' (Wittgenstein), 'multiple realities' (James, Schutz), 'alternate realities' (Castaneda), 'language structures' (Whorf), 'problematics' (Bachelard, Althusser). Each is used to show that in some way the meanings of terms, expressions, or descriptions have to be grasped hermeneutically, that is, in relation to what I shall call generically *frames of meaning*. But the principle of relativity of meaning thus expressed readily threatens to slide into relativism or *radical conventionalism*, in the manner, for instance, of Winch in his attempt to draw upon Wittgenstein in relation to the understanding of alien cultures. Kuhn has consistently withdrawn from the relativistic implications of his account of the development of science, but without successfully spelling out how the process of paradigm transformation can be rendered compatible with a model of scientific 'progress'. For if paradigms are closed systems of epistemological premises, which succeed each other by processes of revolutionary change, how is anyone to be able rationally to adjudge one paradigm against another? This is evidently a duplication of the difficulties arising from the co-existence of discrete language-games in post-Wittgensteinian philosophy.

I shall concentrate here upon the problems raised by Kuhn's *The Structure of Scientific Revolutions*: but most of what I have to say about this applies on a broader level to comparable issues raised by the writings of authors such as those mentioned above. First, Kuhn in that work exaggerates the internal unity of paradigms.[12] The notion of 'paradigm' (notoriously elusive though it turns out to be) refers to taken-for-granted, unexamined assumptions shared by communities of scientists, who confine their attentions to small-scale puzzle-solving within the bounds of those assumptions. But while many scientists, particularly those of an empirical bent, may be ranked as 'normal scientists', in any given period of scientific development the frames within which they work are frequently, and perhaps usually, the subject of deep-rooted division between vying theoretical schools – even if such division is not chronically given expression as articulate controversy. The matters at issue between rival schools are normally rooted in long-standing ontological and epistemological differences which appear and reappear in both the history of philosophy and that of natural science. This connects to the differentiation of paradigms, as frames of scientific theory, from other types of 'forms of life': a potential scepticism regarding the claims of science is in a fundamental sense built into the legitimate order of the social organization of science – even if not constantly acted upon – but is not a feature of religious cosmologies. On the other hand, it is important to remark that a similar error of emphasis, an exaggeration of the internal unity of forms of life, characterizes Winch's discussion. The doctrinal themes that make it possible to speak of 'Christianity' as a single religious cosmology also have been subject to deeply divided differences and struggles of interpretation.

Second, the development of science is constantly interwoven with, and affected by, social influences and interests that nominally stand outside of science itself. Kuhn tends to argue as if 'external' influences come into play only during phases of 'revolutionary' change. But the institutional autonomy of science as critical reason is clearly never more than partial: the dogmatisms as well as the breathtaking innovations in scientific theory are alike conditioned by norms and interests other than those internal to the self-legitimation of science. To say this is not, of course, to suggest that the validity of scientific theories can be reduced to the interests that might play a part in generating them – the classic error in the old 'sociology of knowledge'. But the point definitely needs emphasis – less urgently perhaps in regard to Kuhn's account of the development of the natural sciences than in relation to the philosophies that have generated work such as that of Winch, and which are deeply affiliated to idealistic traditions. The significance of hermeneutics can be properly grasped only if it is stripped away from the traditions of philosophical idealism which generated it.

Third, exaggeration of the internal unity of paradigms means that the latter tend to be treated by Kuhn as 'closed' systems.[13] This leads to a characteristic difficulty in dealing with meaning-variance between paradigms which once more duplicates that manifest on a more general level in the works of various other of the authors to whom I have previously referred. How is it possible to get from one meaning-frame into another, if they are separate and self-enclosed universes? The problem is an insuperable one as it stands; but this is because it is wrongly posed in the first place. Frames of meaning appear as discrete, thus: ( ) ( ) ( ). In lieu of this, we must substitute, as a *starting-point*, that *all paradigms* (read 'language-games', etc.) *are mediated by others*. This is so on the level both of the successive development of paradigms within science, and of the actor's learning to 'find his or her way about' within a paradigm. While Einsteinian physics broke profoundly with Newtonian physics, it none the less had direct continuities with it at the same time; if Protestantism differs in basic ways from Catholicism, the content of the former cannot be fully understood apart from its relation to the latter as critique. The process of learning a paradigm or language-game as the expression of a form of life is also a process of learning what that paradigm is not: that is to say, learning to mediate it with other, rejected alternatives, by contrast to which the claims of the paradigm in question are clarified. This process is itself often embroiled in the struggles over interpretation which result from the internal fragmentation of frames of meaning, and from the fragility of the boundaries that separate what is 'internal' to the frame from what is 'external' to it, that is, belongs to discrete or rival meaning-frames.

Relativism and hermeneutic analysis

If this analysis be accepted, there is no logical difficulty presented by *relativism on the level of meaning*, that is to say, that form of relativism, tending to derive from an overemphasis upon the 'closed' character of frames of meaning, in which the translation of meanings from one frame to another appears as logically impossible. Relativism on the level of meaning can be partially separated from *judgemental relativism*: by this I mean the view that different frames of meaning express distinct 'realities', each of which forms a specific universe of experience that is logically equivalent to any other, and which hence cannot be rationally evaluated in relation to any other but has to be accepted as 'given'. Each of these forms of relativism generates paradoxes; each makes the circle in which all knowledge moves – always involving presuppositions, but being able to illuminate such presuppositions through knowledge built upon them – into a vicious rather a fruitful one. I take it as axiomatic that neither relativism on the level of meaning nor judgemental relativism is able to meet the objection from its own premises. That is to say, there is no way of expressing them which is not self-negating in the manner of all universal claims of the form 'all knowledge is relative'. Familiar and banal as it is, this seems to me a much more conclusive objection to relativism than that which points out that it denies to us the possibility of doing what we know we can do – translate from one language into another, critically analyse the standards of other cultures, talk of 'false consciousness', etc. The possibility of doing these things derives precisely from the rejection of the self-negating character of the relativistic position that starts with a universal claim, and only ends with the discovery that all knowledge moves in a circle.

In order, then, to transcend judgemental relativism it is necessary to sustain a distinction between *sense and reference* in respect of frames of meaning. The mediation of frames of meaning is a hermeneutic problem, whether this concerns the relation between paradigms, within science, or the understanding of distant historical periods or of alien cultures. Hermeneutic analysis demands a respect for the *authenticity* of mediated frames of meaning: this is the necessary avenue for understanding other forms of life, that is, generating descriptions of them that are potentially available to those who have not directly participated in them. But authenticity on the level of meaning has to be distinguished from the validity of propositions about the world that are expressed as beliefs within a particular meaning-frame. This is the distinction between mutual knowledge and common sense that I have made earlier (pp. 121ff). The understanding of Zande witchcraft by a Westerner is a hermeneutic problem involving the mediation of frames of meaning; such an understanding is a condition of, rather than logically excluding, the possibility of, say, comparing the validity of a germ theory of disease with a theory that disease can be induced by rituals of sorcery.

I do not wish to suggest that these comments help to resolve how 'truth' is to be understood, or that they imply a commitment to a correspondence theory. Popper defends a version of the latter, in the guise of Tarski's conception of truth. But there are severe, perhaps insuperable, difficulties with such a view that are very much bound up with the significance of divergences between frames of meaning. Tarski's theory supposedly shows how it is possible to make a statement in a metalanguage of the correspondence of an object language to a factual state of affairs, of the form ' "s" is true if, and only if, s'. But the application of such a notion, even if it is not represented as a *criterion* of truth, seems to presuppose the existence of a neutral observation language in which the claims expressed within two different meaning frames (paradigms or theories) can be formulated in the statement 's'.[14]

In case the point needs re-emphasis, it should be repeated that the assessment of rival theories of disease within the terms of Western science is not and cannot be self-justifying: the commitment to science cannot itself be rationally justified in terms of those criteria that define the rationality of scientific method as such. Arguments which appeal to the superior 'cognitive power' of science will not do, except as documenting the *historical* success of Western science and technology in materially destroying other cultures.

Such an analysis of the philosophy of science does no more than provide an initial approach to the logic and epistemology of the social sciences. We may accept that, as in natural science, in sociology there are no theory-free observations or 'data'; that a scheme of 'sophisticated falsificationism' offers an initial (but not wholly adequate) approach to problems of testability; and that the grasping of any major theoretical perspective, or the mediation of such perspectives, regardless of whether one reserves the term 'paradigm' for the natural sciences or otherwise, are hermeneutic tasks. Beyond this we have to take up a series of issues that stem from the profound differences which separate the social from the natural sciences. Sociology, unlike natural science, stands in a subject–subject relation to its 'field of study', not a subject–object relation; it deals with a pre-interpreted world, in which the meanings developed by active subjects actually enter into the constitution or production of that world; the construction of social theory thus involves a double hermeneutic that has no parallel elsewhere; and finally the logical status of generalizations is in a very significant way distinct from that of natural scientific laws.

Before moving on to these problems, however, it is worth while connecting hermeneutics briefly with the discussion of rationality in Anglo-American philosophy. Beliefs held by members of alien cultures – for example, that a human being may also simultaneously be a raven – have traditionally provided a source of worry for anthropologists. Lévy-Bruhl, at least in the early part of his career, held that 'primitive thought' is 'pre-logical', because it does not recognize a principle of contradiction: for is it not simply self-contradictory to hold that a human being is a human being and yet simultaneously a raven? Yet such a belief is not notably different from beliefs that come from much nearer to home: for example, that the bread broken in communion is the body of Christ and the wine his blood; or that a finite system of mathematics can embrace a concept of infinity; or that increasing velocity lengthens the passing of time. The point is that the mediation of frames of meaning cannot be treated in terms of the premises of formal logic imposed as a set of 'necessary' relations which all thought, to be rational, must observe. Formal logic does not deal in metaphor, irony, sarcasm, deliberate contradiction and other subtleties of language as practical activity. Consider a statement such as 'It is raining, but I don't believe that it is.' Is this necessarily self-contradictory? The answer is that it is not: at least, in certain contexts, there is nothing particularly unusual in a person saying something very close to it. A farmer waking up to rain after a long drought might say 'It's raining. I don't believe it.' Or a woman watching a shower might remark to another: 'Of course this isn't really *rain*.' Now one might respond, when the farmer says he does not believe it, that this is an ironical way of saying that in fact he does believe it; and that there is an implied understanding in the second circumstance ('This is only a minor shower compared to the monsoons that I experienced in the tropics'). But this is precisely the point; and what applies in miniature to such instances applies more macroscopically in, for example, the process of coming to understand the beliefs of an alien culture.[15]

The criteria for the establishment of theoretical meta-languages – precision, abstraction, etc. – are distinct from those of everyday and other forms of non-scientific language. But there is some plausibility in holding that metaphor has an important role in the creation of innovative paradigms. To become acquainted with a new paradigm is to grasp a new frame of meaning, in which familiar premises are altered: elements of the novel scheme are learned through metaphorical allusion to the old. Metaphor both produces and expresses what Schon calls a 'displacement of concepts': the connection of disparate frames in a way which is initially 'unusual'. Metaphor is perhaps thus at the heart of innovations of language, so that there is an essential poetics in the succession of scientific theories which reflects and draws upon the metaphysical usages of natural language.

Some clarification of these points may still be necessary. The implication is not that hermeneutics dispenses with the notions of identity and contradiction; but that the modes whereby these are expressed within divergent frames of meaning have to be grasped contextually, as elements of the practice of particular forms of life. Consider the talk of a schizophrenic. To dismiss such speech as not *authentic* might be the characteristic approach of a behaviouristic psychiatrist. But if, as some claim, schizophrenic talk is a transposed form of ordinary speech, schizophrenic thought and action can be understood as an authentic frame of meaning, thus establishing the possibility of dialogue between schizophrenic and therapist.

What applies to consistencies within frames of meaning, however, also applies to *inconsistencies*, and *disputed or contested meanings*: that is, these too have to be grasped hermeneutically.

The problem of adequacy

The social sciences are not the only fields of endeavour whose object is to 'understand' human conduct; they share such an aim with literature and the arts. Literary and artistic forms, of course, are not infrequently inspired by nature, and by natural events in which human activity plays no role. But, for the most part, where nature enters in, it is humanized nature: the interchange between human activity and the natural environment. For the arts, in every culture, are above all concerned with human being themselves: with their place in the universe, their relation to gods and spirits, the characteristics of the human condition. Such portrayals of human life are bound to the reflexive capacity of human beings to reconstruct imaginatively, and develop an emotional relation towards, experiences that are not their own; and thereby to further their understanding of themselves. This reminds us of the closeness of the connections between the arts and the social sciences, which are basically twofold. First, both draw upon the resources of mutual knowledge in order to develop a dialogue whereby the self-understanding of the reader may be furthered through new understandings of others. Second, both the arts and the social sciences are of necessity deeply involved in a creative mediation of forms of life. The arts are not limited by the demand to provide a 'veridical' description of anything in reality, and since this allows them creative powers that are denied social science by its very format, there is in this a definite tension between the two. Social scientific analyses are rarely likely to yield the dramatic impact that it is possible to attain through imaginative literature or poetic symbolism. But the significance of this should not be exaggerated. Thus Goffman's analyses of 'staged performances', for example, draw from, and appeal to, mutual knowledge; and by comparing all sorts of activities, from the most elevated to the most humble, to such performances, the author is able to achieve the sort of deflationary effect which comes from turning an existing order of things upside down, and which is such a prominent theme in comedy and farce.

Generating descriptions of social conduct as a topic for sociological analysis depends upon the immersion of the observer in a form of life, whereby the hermeneutic mediation of language-games can be accomplished. But how are we to take 'immersion' here? It evidently cannot be understood as equivalent to 'full membership'. An anthropologist who visits an alien culture does not, with a deepening knowledge of that culture, sacrifice her or his original identity: the specific task of anthropology, indeed, is that of mediating the description of the one in the terms of the other. To 'get to know' a form of life is to be able to find one's way about in it: that is to say, to possess the mutual knowledge necessary to sustain encounters with others, regardless of whether this capacity is actually employed. Two further questions arise. First, it is clear that the capacity to sustain encounters can only be adjudged as 'adequate' in relation to the responses, or projected responses, of lay members in so far as they are prepared to accept what the observer does or says as 'authentic' or 'typical'. How are we to specify more precisely what this involves? Second, what is the connection between the hermeneutic task of the mediation of descriptions of forms of life and the technical concepts developed in the social sciences? These are twin aspects of what Schutz, following Weber, refers to as the 'problem of adequacy'.

Winch, like Schutz, recognizes that the social sciences may legitimately employ concepts that are not familiar to those to whose behaviour they refer. Winch mentions the notion of 'liquidity preference' in economics, saying, however, that it is logically tied to concepts business people use in their activities, 'for its use by the economist presupposes his understanding of what it is to conduct a business, which in turn involves an understanding of such business concepts as money, cost, risk, etc.'[16] He says little beyond this, and in his account it is clear neither what this 'logical tie' is nor, as I have said in discussing his writings, what point there is in employing a technical vocabulary in sociology or the other social sciences at all, given that their explanatory relevance is supposedly limited to explicating the intelligibility of action. In a passage immediately following that referred to above, Winch argues that it is only the relation between the economist's 'liquidity preference' and actors' concepts of 'money, cost, risk, etc.' which makes the activity referred to 'economic' rather than, say, 'religious'. But that matters are not as simple as this can be readily seen by taking just this example. A ceremonial in which someone adorns a place of worship with gold to propitiate a god is regarded both by that individual and by an observer as a religious activity; but the observer may also surely quite sensibly characterize what the actor does as an 'investment of funds'. One can go further: there may be characterizations of an actor's conduct that he or she may not only find unfamiliar, but might actively refuse to recognize as valid if presented with them. The latter circumstance is certainly not a sufficient basis in and of itself to reject them, although how far the person 'understands' them, or can be helped to understand them, and how far she or he accepts them is very often likely to be *relevant* to adjudging their accuracy.

To clarify these problems, we must retrace our steps somewhat. Interaction is the product of the constituting skills of human agents. 'Ordinary language' plays a fundamental role in the constitution of interaction both as a medium of the *description* (characterization) of acts and as a medium of *communication* between actors, these normally being closely interwoven with one another in the practical activities of everyday life; hence the use of language *itself* is a practical activity. The generation of descriptions of acts by everyday actors is not incidental to social life as ongoing *Praxis*, but is absolutely integral to its production and inseparable from it, since the characterization of what others do, and more narrowly their intentions and reasons for what they do, is what makes possible the intersubjectivity through which the transfer of communicative intent is realized. It is in these terms that *Verstehen* must be conceived of: not as a special method of entry to the social world peculiar to the social sciences, but as the ontological condition of human society as it is produced and reproduced by its members. The centrality of natural language to both the constituting of action as 'meaningful' and the process of communication in interaction is therefore such that recourse to it is necessary in the generation of any sort of 'research materials' in sociology: the sociological observer cannot construct a technical metalanguage that is unconnected with the categories of natural language (it *may* be true, for somewhat different reasons, that a natural scientific observer cannot either: cf. Polanyi on the role of 'tacit knowledge' in the framing of observations, and the discussion of Gödel's theorem in the framing of theories. But this is controversial in a way in which it cannot be in the social sciences, which deal with a world which is already 'interpreted' by its constituent subjects, who constitute it *as* a world for study through sustaining it as 'meaningful'). We have to separate out the consequences of this (1) for sociological *method*, and (2) for the construction of metalanguages of social analysis or theory.

1 All types of social and historical research demand communication, in some sense, with the persons or collectivities that are the 'subject-matter' of that research. In some instances – participant observation, the use of questionnaires, interviews and the rest – this occurs as actual interaction between observer and subject. But whether this is direct or, as in historical work, indirect, the study of human social conduct depends upon the mastery of mutual knowledge, which poses hermeneutic problems to the observer to the degree to which the object of study is embroiled in unfamiliar forms of life. Now it is crucial to hermeneutic analysis to recognize that the practical reasoning and interpretative schemes employed in day-to-day life in Western culture, or more generally in other cultures not penetrated by the rationality of Western science, are not obliged to conform to the 'law of the excluded middle', to the oppositions of sense as formulated abstractly in a lexicon, or to ideals of abstraction and precision. This does not imply that such schemes do not necessarily have a logical structure involving principles of identity and contradiction. They must have if they are to be 'understandable' on the level of meaning at all; but these do not have to be 'sought for' within the frame of meaning itself, and are not necessarily immediately apparent in terms of the demarcations of identity and contradiction involved in either the natural language of the analyst or in any sociological metalanguage. They may also be frequently (*necessarily* not universally) violated, producing logical contradictions *in their own terms*.

2 The mediation of hermeneutic analysis is bound neither to the *substance*, or 'propositional content', of a frame of meaning, nor to its particular *logical form*. The former point is recognized by every anthropologist who states of his or her observations of a ritual that 'the *x believe* that their dance will bring rain', but is quite happy to say of another of their activities 'the *x* grow their crops by planting seeds every autumn.' The second point is

that which Schutz was presumably getting at in distinguishing between 'rational constructs of models of human action' on the one hand and 'constructs of models of rational human actions' on the other. One can discuss ambiguity without ambiguity. Sociological concepts that refer to meaningful conduct, that is, where concepts used by actors themselves are a medium whereby interaction is accomplished, have to 'pick up' the differentiations of meaning which are relevant to that accomplishment, but are in *no way* constrained to embody the same differentiations in their own formulation. This is the significance of the double hermeneutic in the construction of theoretical metalanguages in sociology. Thus the notion of 'liquidity preference' presumes that actors are able to make the differentiations of 'price', 'cost', 'selling', etc., whereby 'business activity' is brought into being and sustained (not of course as notions that the relevant actors can necessarily easily explicate or give a verbal account of), but at the same time introduces classes of differentiations unknown to those actors. This applies not only to neologisms introduced by sociological observers, but to notions in ordinary language used in technical senses (for example, 'reason', 'cause'), in which the claim must be that the reformulation both presumes yet 'improves upon' – in terms of criteria of precision, etc. – its use in day-to-day life.

Every competent social actor is herself or himself a social theorist, who as a matter of routine makes interpretations of her or his own conduct, and of the intentions, reasons and motives of others as integral to the production of social life. Hence there is necessarily a reciprocal relation between the concepts employed by members of society and those used by sociological observers, or coined by them as neologisms. This is of decisive importance in social science, although the positivistic apparatus of most schools of 'orthodox' sociology has obscured it. Herein lies the pathos of nineteenth-century social thought as represented by the line of development through Comte to Durkheim, and that through certain readings of Marx to the determinism of Marxism-Leninism. For the extension of natural science to the study of social life was undertaken with the promise of liberating human beings from their bondage to forces perceived only dimly or in mystified form. Yet that knowledge discloses that we are in the thrall of 'external' societal causes which bring about mechanically events that we suppose to be under our rational control; the subject initiating the investigation is rediscovered as an object. In such a perspective the reciprocal relation between social analysis and everyday conduct is represented only in marginal forms, for example, the 'self-fulfilling' or 'self-negating prophecy': awareness of a prediction about their conduct on the part of actors can serve to fulfil the prediction or to ensure its failure.

I shall not enter here into the difficult and controversial matter of the logical form of causal laws in natural science. But however this be conceived, it seems clear that causal generalizations in the natural sciences presuppose a set of invariant relations, expressed either in terms of probabilities or as universal connections. All such generalizations involve conditions, and hence even universal laws can in a certain sense be modified by human intervention in nature: the temperature at which water boils in a container can be altered by changing the air pressure, although this in no way affects the law itself. In structural analysis in the social sciences, on the other hand, the causal relations which theoretical generalizations express do not refer to mechanical connections established in nature, but to the outcomes of human doings; this applies to generalizations in economics which concern the distribution of material goods just as much as it does to those which are formulated in the other social sciences. As such, they are the reproduced unintended consequences of intended acts, and are *malleable in the light of the development of human knowledge*. It does not follow from this that the connection between inputs of knowledge and the modification of those conditions in which human beings appear as objects to themselves is a simple one, necessarily expanding human autonomy. In the first place, such conditions may be altered by 'self-knowledge' which is false just as much by that which is valid. Second, the expansion of knowledge concerning the circumstances of human action occurs not in regard of human action in the abstract but within a differentiated society, in which only some might have access to it. Third, rational 'self-understanding' is not the same as 'autonomy'. A slave who fully comprehends the circumstances of his or her own subordination may nevertheless remain a slave. Yet it is fundamental to recognize that 'objective' causal conditions that influence human action can in principle be recognized and incorporated into that action in such a way as to transform it.

This observation concerns features of human activity that bear only a superficial resemblance to indeterminacy in physics. It is sometimes argued that self-fulfilling and self-negating predictions do not present a 'difficulty' unique to the social sciences, since in natural science also observations made about a series of events may influence the course of those events. However, in social science, 'indeterminacy' – a poor term in this connection – results from the incorporation of knowledge as a means to the securing of outcomes in purposeful conduct. Self-influencing observations or predictions represent one aspect of a much more far-reaching phenomenon in sociology than is true of natural science.

Conclusion: Some New Rules of Sociological Method

At this point I shall recapitulate some of the themes of this brief study and try to draw some of the threads together. The schools of 'interpretative sociology' which I discussed in chapter 1 have made some essential contributions to the clarification of the logic and method of the social sciences. In summary form, these are the following: the social world, unlike the world of nature, has to be grasped as a skilled accomplishment of active human subjects; the constitution of this world as 'meaningful', 'accountable' or 'intelligible' depends upon language, regarded, however, not simply as a system of signs or symbols but as a medium of practical activity; the social scientist of necessity draws upon the same sorts of skills as those whose conduct he or she seeks to analyse in order to describe it; generating descriptions of social conduct depends upon the hermeneutic task of penetrating the frames of meaning which lay actors themselves draw upon in constituting and reconstituting the social world.

These insights, however, derive from schools of thought which stand close to philosophical idealism and manifest the traditional shortcomings of that philosophy when transferred to the field of social analysis: a concern with 'meaning' to the exclusion of the practical involvements of human life in material activity (for while it is true that human beings do not produce the world of nature, they do none the less produce from it, and actively transform the conditions of their own existence by so doing); a tendency to seek to explain all human conduct in terms of motivating ideals at the expense of the causal conditions of action; and a failure to examine social norms in relation to asymmetries of power and divisions of interest in society. These shortcomings cannot be rectified within the traditions of thought in which they originate, but nor can the positive contributions which they go along with be readily accommodated within rival theoretical schemes that have translated human agency into social determinism, and which have retained strong associations with positivism in philosophy. Three interlacing orders of problems have to be resolved in order to transcend the limitations of interpretative sociologies, concerning: the clarification of the concept of action and the correlate notions of intention, reason and motive; the connecting of the theory of action to the analysis of the properties of institutional structures; and the epistemological difficulties which confront any attempt to elucidate the logic of social-scientific method.

The failure of the Anglo-American philosophy of action to develop a concern with institutional analysis is reflected in an overconcentration upon purposive conduct. Thus many authors have been inclined to assimilate 'action' with 'intended action', and 'meaningful act' with 'intended outcome'; and they have not been much interested in analysing the origins of the purposes that actors endeavour to realize, which are assumed as given, or the unintended consequences that courses of purposive action serve to bring about. Freeing the concept of action as such, and the identification of the meaning of acts, from any necessary connection with intentions distances the hermeneutic tasks of social science from subjectivism, and makes possible a clarification both of the nature of the causal conditions of action and of the double hermeneutic with which the social sciences are inevitably involved.

'Intention', 'reason' and 'motive', I have argued, are all potentially misleading terms, since they already presuppose a conceptual 'cutting into' the continuity of action, and are aptly treated as expressing an ongoing reflexive monitoring of conduct that 'competent' actors are expected to maintain as a routine part of their day-to-day lives. The reflexive monitoring of conduct only becomes the statement of intentions, or the giving of reasons, either when actors carry out retrospective enquiries into their own conduct or, more usually, when queries about their behaviour are made by others. The rationalization of action is closely bound up with the moral evaluations of 'responsibility' which actors make of each other's conduct, and hence with moral norms and the sanctions to which those who contravene them are subject; thus spheres of 'competence' are defined in law as what every citizen is 'expected to know about' and take account of in monitoring his or her action.

Orthodox functionalism, as represented most prominently by Durkheim and later by Parsons, does embody an attempt to connect intentional action and institutional analysis, via the theorem that the moral values upon which social solidarity rests also appear as motivating elements in personality. This view, I have tried to show, serves only to replace the notion of action with the thesis that the properties of social and personality systems have to be examined in conjunction with one another: the member of society does not figure here as a skilled, creative agent, capable of reflexively monitoring his or her behaviour (and in principle capable of doing so in the light of anything she or he may believe can be learned from Parsons's theories!).

I have therefore set out an alternative view, one capable of more detailed development, but whose outlines should be clear. The production of society is brought about by the active constituting skills of its members, but draws upon resources, and depends upon conditions, of which they are unaware or which they perceive only dimly. Three aspects of the production of interaction can be distinguished: the constitution of meaning, morality and relations of power. The means whereby these are brought into being can also be regarded as modalities of the reproduction of structure: the idea of the duality of structure is a central one here, since structure appears as both condition and consequence of the production of interaction. All organizations or collectivities 'consist of' systems of interaction, and can be analysed in terms of their structural properties: but as systems, their existence depends upon modes of structuration whereby they are reproduced. The reproduction of modes of domination, one must emphasize, expresses asymmetries in the forms of meaning and morality that are made to 'count' in interaction, thus tying them in to divisions of interest that serve to orient struggles over divergent interpretations of frames of meaning and moral norms.

The production of interaction as 'meaningful', I have proposed, can usefully be analysed as depending upon 'mutual knowledge' which is drawn upon by participants as interpretative schemes to make sense of what each other says and does. Mutual knowledge is not corrigible to the sociological observer, who must draw upon it just as lay actors do in order to generate descriptions of their conduct; in so far as such 'knowledge', however, can be represented as 'common sense', as a series of factual beliefs, it is in principle open to confirmation or otherwise in the light of social scientific analysis.

Some aspects of the philosophy of natural science, I have argued, are relevant to elucidating the logical status of claims to knowledge made in the social sciences. But their relevance is limited by features which have no immediate parallel in the natural sciences; and in any case such developments themselves have to be subjected to critical scrutiny. Kuhn's use of the term 'paradigm' shares important elements with other versions of the notion of what I have called 'frame of meaning', and as Kuhn applies it to analysing the history of science, also raises similar difficulties to these other versions. Thus Kuhn exaggerates the internal unity of 'paradigms', as Winch does 'forms of life', and consequently does not acknowledge that the problem of the mediation of different frames of meaning has to be treated as the *starting-point* of analysis. When conjoined to an insistence upon a distinction of sense and reference, this allows us to grasp the significance of the hermeneutic recognition of the authenticity of meaning-frames without slipping into a relativism which forecloses the possibility of any rational evaluation of them. The mediation of paradigms or widely discrepant theoretical schemes in science is a hermeneutic matter like that involved in the contacts between other types of meaning-frame.

Sociology, unlike natural science, deals with a pre-interpreted world, where the creation and reproduction of meaning-frames is a very condition of that which it seeks to analyse, namely human social conduct: this is, to repeat, why there is a double hermeneutic in the social sciences that poses as a specific difficulty what Schutz, following Weber, calls the 'postulate of adequacy'. I have suggested that Schutz's formulation of this, based upon the thesis that the technical concepts of social science have to be in some way capable of being reduced to lay notions of everyday action, will not do. It has in fact to be reversed: rather than, in some sense, the concepts of sociology having to be open to rendition in terms of lay concepts, it is the case that the observing social scientist has to be able first to grasp those lay concepts, that is, penetrate hermeneutically the form of life whose features he or she wishes to analyse or explain.

The relation between technical vocabularies of social science and lay concepts is a shifting one: just as social scientists adopt everyday terms – 'meaning', 'motive', 'power', etc. – and use them in specialized senses, so lay actors tend to take over the concepts and theories of the social sciences and embody them as constitutive elements in the rationalization of their own conduct. The significance of this phenomenon is recognized only marginally in orthodox sociology, in the guise of 'self-fulfilling' or 'self-negating' prophecies, which are regarded simply as nuisances that inhibit accurate prediction. Yet although causal generalizations in the social sciences in some aspects may resemble natural scientific laws, they are in an essential way distinct from the latter because they depend upon reproduced alignments of unintended consequences; in so far as they are announced as generalizations, and are picked up as such by those to whose conduct they apply, their form is altered. This once more reunites us with the theme of reflexivity, central to this study. Social science stands in a relation of tension to its 'subject-matter' – as a potential instrument of the expansion of *rational autonomy of action*, but equally as a potential *instrument of domination*.

In conclusion, and in summary form, here are some new 'rules of sociological method'. The latter phrase is only intended ironically. I do not claim that the presuppositions that follow are 'rules' in the sense in which I have suggested that term is most appropriately used in the social sciences. Rather, they are a skeletal statement of some of the themes of the study as a whole, and are merely designed to exemplify its differences from the famous sociological manifesto that Durkheim issued almost a century ago. This statement does not in and of itself constitute a 'programme' for sociological research, although I regard it as an integral part of such a programme. The sub-classification provided below works roughly as follows. Section A concerns the 'subject-matter of sociology': the production and reproduction of society; section B, the boundaries of agency, and the modes in which processes of production and reproduction may be examined; section C, the modes in which social life is 'observed' and characterizations of social activity established; section D, the formulation of concepts within the meaning-frames of social science as metalanguages.

A

1 *Sociology is not concerned with a 'pre-given' universe of objects, but with one which is constituted or produced by the active doings of subjects.* Human beings transform nature socially, and by 'humanizing' it they transform themselves; but they do not, of course, produce the natural world, which is constituted as an object-world independently of their existence. If in transforming that world they create history, and thence live *in* history, they do so because the production and reproduction of society is not 'biologically programmed', as it is among the lower animals. (Theories human beings develop may, through their technological applications, affect nature, but they cannot come to constitute features *of* the natural world as they do in the case of the social world.)

2 *The production and reproduction of society thus has to be treated as a skilled performance on the part of its members*, not as merely a mechanical series of processes. To emphasize this, however, is definitely not to say that actors are wholly aware of what these skills are, or just how they manage to exercise them; or that the forms of social life are adequately understood as the intended outcomes of action.

B

1 *The realm of human agency is bounded. Human beings produce society, but they do so as historically located actors,*

and not under conditions of their own choosing. There is an unstable margin, however, between conduct that can be analysed as intentional action, and behaviour that has to be analysed nomologically as a set of 'occurrences'. In respect of sociology, the crucial task of nomological analysis is to be found in the explanation of the structural properties of social systems.

2 *Structure must not be conceptualized as simply placing constraints upon human agency, but as enabling.* This is what I call the *duality of structure*. Structure can always in principle be examined in terms of its *structuration*. To enquire into the structuration of social practices is to seek to explain how it comes about that structure is constituted through action, and reciprocally how action is constituted structurally.

3 *Processes of structuration involve an interplay of meanings, norms and power.* These three concepts are analytically equivalent as the 'primitive' terms of social science, and *are logically implicated in both the notion of intentional action and that of structure*: every cognitive and moral order is at the same time a system of power, involving a 'horizon of legitimacy'.

C

1 *The sociological observer cannot make social life available as a 'phenomenon' for observation independently of drawing upon her or his knowledge of it as a resource whereby it is constituted as a 'topic for investigation'.* In *this* respect, the observer's position is no different from that of any other member of society; 'mutual knowledge' is not a series of corrigible items, but represents the interpretative schemes which both sociologists and lay actors use, and must use, to 'make sense' of social activity – that is, to generate 'recognizable' characterizations of it.

2 *Immersion in a form of life is the necessary and only means whereby an observer is able to generate such characterizations.* 'Immersion' here – say, in relation to an alien culture – does not, however, mean 'becoming a full member' of the community, and cannot mean this. To 'get to know' an alien form of life is to know how to find one's way about in it, to

be able to participate in it as an ensemble of practices. But for the sociological observer this is a mode of generating descriptions which have to be mediated, that is, transformed into categories of social-scientific discourse.

D

1 *Sociological concepts thus obey a double hermeneutic*:
   (a)   Any theoretical scheme in the natural or social sciences is in a certain sense a form of life in itself, the concepts of which have to be mastered as a mode of practical activity generating specific types of descriptions. That this is already a hermeneutic task is clearly demonstrated in the philosophy of science of Kuhn and others.
   (b)   Sociology, however, deals with a universe which is already constituted within frames of meaning by social actors themselves, and reinterprets these within its own theoretical schemes, mediating ordinary and technical language. This double hermeneutic is of considerable complexity, since the connection is not merely a one-way one; there is a continual 'slippage' of the concepts constructed in sociology, whereby these are appropriated by those whose conduct they were originally coined to analyse, and hence tend to become integral features *of* that conduct (thereby in fact potentially compromising their original usage within the technical vocabulary of social science).
2 *In sum, the primary tasks of sociological analysis are the following*:
   (a)   *The hermeneutic explication and mediation of divergent forms of life within descriptive metalanguages of social science;*
   (b)   *Explication of the production and reproduction of society as the accomplished outcome of human agency.*

Notes

Introduction to the second edition

1 Giddens, Anthony, *The Constitution of Society*, Cambridge, 1984.
2 Mouzelis, Nicos, *Back to Sociological Theory: The construction of social orders*, London, 1991; Harbers, Hans, and de Vries, Gerard, 'Empirical consequences of the "double hermeneutic"', *Social Epistemology*, Vol. 6, 1992.
3 Mouzelis, *Back to Sociological Theory*, pp. 27–8.
4 Ibid., p. 35.
5 cf. Giddens, *The Consequences of Modernity*, Cambridge, 1990.
6 This point is accepted by Mouzelis. Mouzelis, *Back to Sociological Theory*, pp. 32–4.
7 Giddens, *The Consequences of Modernity*.
8 Knorr-Cetina, Karen, 'Social and scientific method or what do we make of the distinction between the natural and social sciences?', *Philosophy of the Social Sciences*, Vol. 2, 1981.
9 Harbers and de Vries, 'Empirical consequences of the "double hermeneutic"', p. 4.
10 Ibid., p. 11.
11 Lynch, William T., 'What does the double hermeneutic explain/justify?', *Social Epistemology*, Vol. 6, 1992.
12 Ibid., p. 16.
13 Ibid., p. 38.

Chapter 1 Some schools of social theory and philosophy

1 Schutz's *Der sinnhafte Aufbau der sozialen Welt* appeared in Germany in 1932. Translated as *The Phenomenology of the Social World* (London, 1972), the book was first published in English in 1967.

2 Ryle, Gilbert, 'Phenomenology', *Collected Papers*, Vol. I, London, 1971, p. 176. See also the following essay, 'Phenomenology versus the concept of mind'. Compare Wittgenstein, *Zettel*, Oxford, 1967, § 401–2.

3 Sartre, Jean-Paul, *L'Être et le néant*, Paris, 1950, p. 47.

4 Schutz, Alfred, 'On multiple realities', *Collected Papers*, Vol. 2, The Hague, 1967, p. 229.

5 Schutz, *Phenomenology of the Social World*, p. 8.

6 Ibid., pp. 92–3.

7 Schutz, *Reflections on the Problem of Relevance*, New Haven, 1970, pp. 33ff.

8 Ibid., p. 120.

9 'Our everyday thoughts are less interested in the antithesis "true–false" than in the sliding transition "likely–unlikely" . . . To this extent, but only to this extent, the principle of pragmatism is incontestably well founded. It is a description of the style of everyday thought, but not a theory of cognition.' 'The problem of rationality in the social world', *Collected Papers*, Vol. 2, pp. 76–7.

10 'Common-sense and scientific interpretation of human action', *Collected Papers*, Vol. 1, pp. 36ff.

11 *Phenomenology of the Social World*, p. 220.

12 'Common-sense and scientific interpretation of human action', p. 44.

13 Ibid., pp. 9 and 37.

14 Ibid., pp. 99, 134, 12 and 208.

15 *Phenomenology of the Social World*, p. 97.

16 Ibid., p. 91.

17 Ibid., p. 93.

18 The first being signalled by the work of Moore, Russell and the early Wittgenstein. Cf. Ayer, A. J., et al., *The Revolution in Philosophy*, London, 1956.

19 Garfinkel, Harold, *Studies in Ethnomethodology*, New Jersey, 1967, p. ix.

20 'The rational properties of scientific and common sense activities', reprinted in the above work. Cf. Elliot, Henry C., 'Similarities and

differences between science and common sense', in Turner, Roy, *Ethnomethodology*, London, 1974.

21 *Studies in Ethnomethodology*, p. 272.

22 Ibid., p. 1.

23 Wittgenstein, Ludwig, *Philosophical Investigations*, Oxford, 1972, p. 146.

24 Bar-Hillel, Yehoshva, 'Indexical expressions', in *Aspects of Language*, Jerusalem, 1970, p. 76.

25 *Studies in Ethnomethodology*, p. 8.

26 Garfinkel, Harold, and Sacks, Harvey, 'On formal structures of practical actions', in McKinney, John C., and Tiryakian, Edward A., *Theoretical Sociology, Perspectives and Developments*, New York, 1970.

27 Ibid., p. 348.

28 Searle, John R., *Speech Acts*, Cambridge, 1969, p. 16.

29 *Studies in Ethnomethodology*, p. viii.

30 Garfinkel, Harold, 'Studies of the routine grounds of everyday activities', in Sudnow, David, *Studies in Social Interaction*, New York, 1972, p. 2.

31 *Studies in Ethnomethodology*, p. 280.

32 Cicourel, Aaron V., *Cognitive Sociology*, London, 1973, p. 124.

33 'On formal structures of practical actions', pp. 338–9.

34 Mates, B., 'On the verification of statements about ordinary language', in Lyas, Colin, *Philosophy and Linguistics*, London, 1971, p. 128.

35 Louch, A. R., *Explanation and Human Action*, Oxford, 1966, p. 175.

36 Ibid., p. 160.

37 Quotations in this and the previous paragraph are from Winch, Peter, *The Idea of a Social Science*, London, 1958, pp. 52, 88 and 123.

38 In particular, in 'Understanding a primitive society', *American Philosophical Quarterly*, Vol. I, 1964.

39 Wittgenstein, Ludwig, *Remarks on the Foundations of Mathematics*, Oxford, 1956, Part 2, §77.

40 'Understanding a primitive society', p. 322.

41 MacIntyre, Alasdair, 'The idea of a social science', *Aristotelian Society Supplement*, Vol. 41, 1967.

42 *The Idea of a Social Science*, p. 40; compare Wittgenstein, *The Blue and Brown Books*, Oxford, 1972, pp. 14ff.

43 Cf. Wittgenstein, *Philosophical Investigations*, Oxford, 1968, §198ff.

44 Schutz, 'Common-sense and scientific interpretation of human action', p. 56.

45 Gadamer, Hans-Georg, *Kleine Schriften*, Vol. I, Tübingen, 1967, p. 109; see also his introduction to the compendious *Das Problem der Sprache*, Munich, 1967.
46 Abel, Theodore, 'The operation called *Verstehen*', *American Journal of Sociology*, Vol. 54, 1948, p. 218.
47 Gadamer, *Wahrheit und Methode*, Tübingen, 1960, pp. 275ff.
48 Heidegger, Martin, *Being and Time*, Oxford, 1967.
49 Gadamer, *Wahrheit und Methode*, p. 362.
50 Ibid., p. 451.
51 Ibid., p. 419.
52 Apel, Karl-Otto, Analytical Philosophy of Language and *the Geisteswissenschaften*, Dordrecht, 1967, p. 39.
53 Wellmer, Albrecht, *Critical Theory of Society*, New York, 1972, p. 30.
54 *Knowledge and Human Interests*, London, 1972, p. 214.
55 Ricoeur, Paul, *Freud and Philosophy*, New Haven, 1970, p. 3.
56 Gadamer, *Wahrheit und Methode*, p. 465.
57 'Toward a theory of communicative competence', in Dreitzel, Hans Peter, *Recent Sociology No. 2*, New York, 1970, p. 138.
58 'A postscript to "Knowledge and Human Interests"', *Philosophy of the Social Sciences*, Vol. 3, 1973, p. 166.
59 *Legitimation Crisis*, Boston, 1975, p. 13.
60 *Theory and Practice*, London, 1971, pp. 28ff.

Chapter 2   Agency, act-identifications and communicative intent

1 Peters, R. S., *The Concept of Motivation*, London, 1958, pp. 12–13.
2 See Danto, Arthur, *Analytical Philosophy of Action*, Cambridge, 1973, pp. 28ff.
3 Austin, J. L., 'Three ways of spilling ink', *The Philosophical Review*, Vol. 75, 1966.
4 Toulmin, Stephen, 'Reasons and causes', in Borger, Robert, and Cioffi, Frank, *Explanation in the Behavioural Sciences*, Cambridge, 1970, p. 12.
5 Davidson, Donald, 'Agency', in Binkley, Robert, et al., *Agent, Action, and Reason*, Oxford, 1971.
6 In talking of the 'production of society', I do not follow Touraine, who has used the same phrase, although only in relation to what he calls the 'sujet historique'. Touraine, Alain, *Production de la société*, Paris, 1973.

7   See, for instance, Shwayder, D. S., *The Stratification of Behaviour*, London, 1965, p. 134; also the same author's 'Topics on the backgrounds of action', *Inquiry*, Vol. 13, 1970.

8   Anscombe, G. E. M., *Intention*, Oxford, 1963, pp. 12ff.

9   Cf. Harré, R., and Secord, P. F., *The Explanation of Social Behaviour*, Oxford, 1972, pp. 159ff.

10   In this respect I agree with Danto, who says: 'A man may do something because he intends to do it, without it following that he wants to: unless we adjust the meaning of "want" so as to make it finally mean just what intention means'. *Analytical Philosophy of Action*, p. 186.

11   Grice, H. P., 'Meaning', *Philosophical Review*, Vol. 66, 1957, p. 385.

12   Grice, 'Utterer's meaning and intentions', *Philosophical Review*, Vol. 78, 1969.

13   Schiffer, Stephen R., *Meaning*, Oxford, 1972, pp. 30–42.

14   Ibid., pp. 1–5 and *passim*.

15   Lewis, David K., *Convention*, Cambridge (Mass.), 1969.

Chapter 3   The production and reproduction of social life

1   Giddens, Anthony, 'The "individual" in the writings of Emile Durkheim', *Archives européennes de sociologie*, Vol. 12, 1971.

2   McHugh, Peter, et al., *On the Beginning of Social Enquiry*, pp. 25 and 27 (my italics).

3   *The Structure of Social Action*, New York, 1949.

4   *The Social System*, London, 1951, p. 81.

6   I think this comment also applies to the analysis developed in Berger, Peter L., and Luckmann, Thomas, *The Social Construction of Reality*, London 1967, which in my opinion quite fails in its attempt to reconcile a theory of action with one of institutional organization.

7   See Giddens, 'Classical social theory and the origins of modern sociology', *American Journal of Sociology*, Vol. 82, 1976.

8   Giddens, 'The "individual" in the writings of Emile Durkheim'.

9   See the Introduction to Giddens, *Emile Durkheim: Selected Writings*, Cambridge, 1972, pp. 38–48.

10   Parsons, Talcott, translator's footnote in Weber, Max, *The Theory of Social and Economic Organisation*, London, 1964, p. 124. Cf. *The Social System*, p. 36, where Parsons distinguishes two aspects of the 'problem of order': the 'Hobbesian problem', and the

problem of 'order in the symbolic systems which make communication possible'.

11 *The German Ideology*, Moscow, 1968, p. 42.

12 Ibid., p. 32.

13 Merleau-Ponty, Maurice, *In Praise of Philosophy*, Evanston, 1963, p. 54.

14 Cf. Goffman on puns, riddles, jokes, etc.: 'Wordplay seems to celebrate the power of the context to disqualify all but one reading, more than it disconfirms the workings of this force.' Goffman, Erving, *Frame Analysis*, New York, 1974, p. 443.

15 Ziff, Paul, 'Natural and formal languages', in Hook, Sidney, *Language and Philosophy*, New York, 1969; see also the same author's *Semantic Analysis*, Ithaca, 1960.

16 Polanyi, Michael, *Personal Knowledge*, London, 1958.

17 I borrow this example again from Ziff, 'What is said', in Davidson, Donald, and Harman, Gilbert, *Semantics of Natural Language*, Dordrecht, 1972.

18 Wright, Georg Henrik von, *Norm and Action*, London, 1963.

19 Löwith, Karl, *From Hegel to Nietzsche*, London, 1964, p. 321.

20 *Grundrisse*, p. 265.

21 Weber, Max, *Economy and Society*, New York, Vol. 1, p. 224.

22 Cf. Giddens, ' "Power" in the recent writings of Talcott Parsons', *Sociology*, Vol. 2, 1968.

23 Lefebvre, Henri, *Everyday Life in the Modern World*, London, 1971.

24 Evans-Pritchard, E. E., *Witchcraft, Oracles and Magic among the Azande*, Oxford, 1950.

25 Ricoeur, Paul, 'The model of the text: meaningful action considered as a text', *Social Research*, Vol. 38, 1971, p. 530.

26 Lévi-Strauss, Claude, 'Réponses à quelques questions', *Esprit*, Vol. 31, 1963, p. 633, 'I am ... completely in agreement with M. Ricoeur when he defines – no doubt to criticise it – my position as "a Kantianism without a transcendental subject". This deficiency causes him to have certain reservations, whereas nothing stops me accepting his formulation'.

27 *Capitalism and Modern Social Theory*, Cambridge, 1971, pp. 65ff and *passim*.

Chapter 4   The form of explanatory accounts

1 Durkheim, Emile, *Suicide*, London, 1952, p. 44. MacIntyre points out that this definition makes actors' reasons irrelevant to the

explanation of suicide. Durkheim eliminates the differences between 'doing X intending that Y shall result', and 'doing X knowing that Y will result'. The latter does not differentiate cases in which 'knowledge' is applied as a means to an end. MacIntyre, 'The idea of a social science' (cf. my formulation of 'intentional action', above, pp. 82ff).

2 Feigl, Herbert, 'The "orthodox" view of theories: some remarks in defence as well as critique', in Radner, M., and Winokur, S., *Minnesota Studies in the Philosophy of Science*, Vol. 4, Minneapolis, 1970.

3 Popper, Karl R., 'Two faces of common sense', in *Objective Knowledge*, Oxford, 1972, pp. 60–3; Quine, W. V., *Word and Object*, Cambridge (Mass.), 1964, 'Grades of theoreticity', in Foster, Lawrence, and Swanson, J. W., *Experience and Theory*, London, 1970.

4 Of Bachelard's works perhaps the most relevant are *Le nouvel esprit scientifique*, Paris, 1946; *Le rationalisme appliqué*, Paris, 1949. Canguilhem, G., *Études d'histoire et de philosophie des sciences*, Paris, 1968. 'L'observation scientifique', Bachelard says, 'est toujours une observation polémique'. *Le nouvel esprit scientifique*, p. 12.

5 Kuhn, Thomas, *The Structure of Scientific Revolutions*, Chicago, 1970; 'Reflections on my critics', in Lakatos, Imre, and Musgrave, Alan, *Criticism and the Growth of Knowledge*, Cambridge, 1970; 'Second thoughts on paradigms', in Suppe, Frederick, *The Structure of Scientific Theories*, Urbana, 1974; Lakatos, Imre, 'Criticism and the methodology of scientific research programmes', *Proceedings of the Aristotelian Society*, Vol. 69, 1968; 'Falsification and the methodology of scientific research programmes', in Lakatos and Musgrave, *Criticism and the Growth of Knowledge*; 'History of science and its rational reconstructions', in Buck, R., and Cohen, Robert, *Boston Studies in the Philosophy of Science*, Vol. 8, Dordrecht, 1971 (see also Kuhn: 'Notes on Lakatos', in the same source); 'Popper on demarcation and induction', in Schilpp, Paul A., *The Philosophy of Karl Popper*, Lasalle, 1974. Feyerabend, Paul, 'Problems of empiricism', in Colodny, R., *Beyond the Edge of Certainty*, Englewood Cliffs, 1965; 'Consolations for the specialist', in Lakatos and Musgrave, *Criticism and the Growth of Knowledge*; 'Against method: outline of an anarchistic theory of knowledge', in Radner, and Winokur, *Minnesota Studies in the Philosophy of Science*, Vol. 4; *Against Method*, London, 1975.

6   Adorno, Theodore, *Der Positivismusstreit in der deutschen Soziologie*, Neuwied, 1969.

7   Merton, R. K., *Social Theory and Social Structure*, New York, 1957.

8   *The Structure of Scientific Revolutions*, p. viii.

9   Popper, *Conjectures and Refutations*, London, 1972, pp. 34–6.

10 An example mentioned by Feyerabend: 'Popper's *Objective Knowledge*', *Inquiry*, Vol. 17, 1974, pp. 499–500. One should recall Duhem's thesis that science never tests isolated hypotheses, only groups of hypotheses. Duhem, Pierre, *To Save the Phenomena*, Chicago, 1969.

11 Lakatos, 'Criticism and the methodology of scientific research programmes', pp. 180ff.

12 In subsequent commentaries Kuhn has clarified or amended his previous position in this respect, as in several other important ways. See, for example, 'Reflections on my critics', and particularly 'Second thoughts on paradigms'.

13 On this point, however, as in regard to the internal coherence of paradigms, Kuhn's later position appears more qualified and satisfactory than his earlier one (see note 12, above).

14 See, however, Davidson, Donald, 'In defence of Convention T', in Leblanc, Hugues, *Truth, Syntax and Modality*, Amsterdam, 1973. My remarks at this point, of course, leave aside a series of major problems concerning the formulation of an adequate treatment of the notions of truth and reference. These are taken up more directly in my discussion of positivism in *Studies in Social and Political Theory*, London, 1982.

15 This is in fact well stated by Winch: 'I never of course denied that Zande witchcraft practices involve appeals to what we can understand as standards of rationality. Such appeals also involve behaviour which we can identify as "the recognition of a contradiction". What I was urging, though, was that we should be cautious in how *we* identify the contradiction, which may not be what it would appear to be if we approach it with "scientific" preconceptions.' Winch, 'Comment', in Borger and Cioffi, *Explanation in the Behavioural Sciences*.

16 Winch, *The Idea of a Social Science*, p. 89.

Index